How to Think Like Muhammad Ali

The Paradox of Greatness and the Power of Mental Toughness

By Kevin Mitchell

Aurum
Press

First published in Great Britain
2014 by Aurum Press Ltd
74–77 White Lion Street
Islington
London N1 9PF
www.aurumpress.co.uk

A catalogue record for this book is available from the British
Library.

ISBN 978 1 78131 349 7

1 3 5 7 9 10 8 6 4 2
2014 2016 2018 2017 2015

Typeset in Perpetua by Saxon Graphics Ltd, Derby
Printed by CPI Group (UK) Ltd, Croydon, CR0 4YY

Contents

Introduction
Poets and Polemicists

In so many respects, Muhammad Ali is a mess of contradictions. He is the black superhero who used his wit and charm to leave a psychic bruise on another African-American giant of his sport, Joe Frazier. And he was there for Joe's funeral. He is the one-time philanderer who married four times and, ultimately – after his final walk up the aisle in 1986 – surrendered himself to the care and devotion of Lonnie, who had adored him as a young neighbour in Louisville in the 1960s. He was the soft-faced purveyor of naïf poetry who beguiled presidents and film stars, and was as tough as any hoodlum. He fought for a living, ferociously at times, but would not kill with a gun under his country's flag. He was a creation of the 1960s but as square as his dad. He was worshipped by liberals but had no problem doing business with some of the world's most reactionary leaders, a couple of whom invited him to the White House. He moved across the canvas with all the grace of Nijinsky but was too useless to dance with Imelda Marcos. The list is long.

When Bundini Brown, his muse, said Ali could, 'Float like a butterfly, sting like a bee', he did more than create an aphorism that became part of the language of his era; he described the ultimate boxing enigma – a fighter of beauty and grace who simultaneously helped opponents towards public helplessness with his unforgiving fists. And he did it all with the cheek of a child. Ali has never lost his sense of wonder, a rare quality for anyone exposed to the treachery of the fight game as long as he was.

That all of these qualities coalesced in one man was not so much remarkable, though, as typical; we are all of us a mess of contradictions. And therein, surely, lies the clue to our fascination with Muhammad Ali. He is our champion of being human. We kind of get him: all the good and bad, the hilarious and the tragic. For the millions who find common ground with him – be it in religion, politics, his boxing prowess or just the joy of laughing – the umbilical link is as strong as that of an infant to its mother, cut soon after incubation but never really severed. Very few members of the human race have been able to touch the hearts of millions with their charisma, their self-awareness, their innate genius or all three: Jesus, Shakespeare, Mozart, Gandhi, Nelson Mandela, Muhammad Ali ... name another.

What Ali did best, however, was fight. He touched even an abolitionist's heart, I would wager, with his mastery of a skill that very few people know or even attempt. And right there is another paradox: it is this elemental urge – born of the survival instinct – that forms the bond between Ali and millions, but it is pretty much a one-way deal. While we do not, except in extreme circumstances, need to fight anymore, the deep feeling does not go away; it is just parked under layers of civilising, held together by trepidation and fear of the unknown. Most human beings do not know what it is like to fight, but we know that we like to watch it – or are at least fascinated by the spectacle, even if it simultaneously evinces guilt. While there are many who turn away and find the very notion of physical conflict nauseating, even those sensitive souls are in some way touched by it. It is sinning by proxy, if you want to put a religious spin on the matter. But, pro or anti, guilty or thrilled, the fact remains we let Ali do our fighting for us, just as fighters always have done – on the battlefield or in the boxing ring. And he paid an awful price – one that very few among us would be prepared to pay.

Because it is plain for all to see that Ali now is not what he was then. He has become, through circumstance and inclination, someone entirely different from the entertainer and boxing champion who first captivated the world in the 1960s. Ali made more noise than any athlete of the twentieth century and now, decades after he last threw a punch, he is silenced by an opponent he could never beat. Yet Ali embraces his Parkinson's disease as if he were holding another fighter in a clinch, kidding him to cease his attack by sheer force of charm. What is just as extraordinary is he bears the disease no ill. This grim burden is his fate and destiny, he says, and it serves a purpose: it turns the pity of others into love, resentment into understanding. Parkinson's has rendered the consummate showman of twentieth-century sport as mute as a baby; and the baby just smiles.

In a world riddled with hate, Ali seems immune to the virus. God knows he has had reason to indulge himself in at least occasional animosity towards some of those who have burgled his spirit and his bank account over the years, but there is little evidence of it. And there have been more vultures around him than lesser fighters ever would have known because there was more flesh to pick at on the Ali carcass. Those carrion thieves also saw in him someone blessedly easy to deceive. They took his good humour to mean naivety. They saw softness in his goodness. They saw a fool where stood someone wiser than themselves. It takes a flinty heart to steal from a man with a very giving one. But who won in the end? Who found contentment: thief or victim? Who spread more happiness and received as much and more in return? Ali is far from perfect, of course, and as human as anyone else on the planet; but he is, essentially, honest. He is all of us and he is none of us. And, last time I checked, he was still standing.

There are as many takes on Ali as he threw punches, probably. In retirement, the legend has grown, as legends tend to do. Millions of words have been spent on him (which he would love), and they cover the gamut of opinion and sentiment. Let's take two of them as an example. In 1996, Davis Miller, a writer from the American school of personal journalism, a proud follower of the Jack Kerouac, Hunter S. Thompson, Tom Wolfe lineage, wrote *The Tao of Muhammad Ali*, beginning with something approximating to poetry and a ringing tribute: 'We struggle. Always. We are doing the best that we can. And we dream of transcendence. For me, there was a time when the dream was incarnate.' Miller adds: 'And the dream's name was Muhammad Ali. This is the story of my time spent with that dream.'

You would guess – and not be far wrong – that what follows over the course of 300-plus pages does not constitute a forensic examination of a fighter or a flawed human being, but the celebration of a hero elevated to something of a divine presence. Almost without exception, the reviews of his book were ecstatic. I enjoyed it immensely, with reservations. An interesting mix of insight and adoration, the book sold well around the world, especially in the UK and in the US, its place of origin. Miller adapted it for radio, which the BBC ran in six parts, and its words and spirit have lingered to this day. Miller also wrote a libretto for an operatic version, *Approaching Ali*, which made its world premiere in Washington in 2013 and was scheduled to tour the US in 2015. Not since John L. Sullivan cashed in on his fistic skills as a vaudeville caricature of himself had a fighter's deeds been so completely – and rather excessively – affixed to the wider cultural stage.

Miller first met Ali at a very interesting point in his boxing career, in July 1975, a month after he had toyed with Joe Bugner over fifteen rounds in the Merdeka Stadium, Kuala Lumpur; and three months before the hell Ali can hardly have contemplated, the Thrilla In Manila, against Joe Frazier – the last fight in their trilogy and a candidate for the most brutal heavyweight fight since John L. Sullivan and Jake

Kilrain brought down the curtain on the bare-knuckle era over seventy-five rounds in 1889. What Miller encountered in between Ali's polar experiences of routine defence and life-and-death struggle was a man at peace with himself, a fighter who appeared to him to be in control of his gifts and his thoughts.

They sparred, to use Miller's description of it, the writer hoping to absorb by the osmosis of pain something of his subject's essence. It is a method that has been tried many times before by literary types. Among early scientists in the experiment was the fabled sports writer Paul Gallico, who 'took on' the world heavyweight champion Jack Dempsey in 1922. Jack dumped him on his pretentious backside in a widely publicised exhibition, but afforded Gallico the opportunity to write, 'I found myself on the floor. Everything went sort of black. I held on to the floor with both hands, because the ring and the audience outside were making a complete clockwise revolution, came to a stop and went back again counterclockwise.'

As an insight into the world of combat, Gallico's contribution probably served some purpose beyond the massaging of his own male ego, but the truth of it was that this, like all the others, was not a proper sporting contest. It was a stunt, a piece of sacrificial derring-do by a dilettante writer risking injury by a dangerously strong athlete. But the template had been set.

Most famous in the modern genre of ego fighting was George Plimpton's little stoush with Archie Moore in 1959. Plimpton made a career of participatory journalism but got more than he bargained for when, self-consciously dressed in a *Paris Review* T-shirt (if he'd worn a tutu and ballet shoes he could hardly have looked more absurd), he endured the disdain of Ol' Mongoose for three rounds. The gulf between fighter and writer was made painfully clear to him. The ageless Moore, who at that stage of his career had knocked out 123 opponents and was the long-reigning world light-heavyweight champion, was not best pleased that the posh Mr Plimpton reckoned this was an exercise in legitimate journalism, and bloodied his features with some stiff blows to his patrician snout. Still, Plimpton had enough material to write his hugely entertaining book, *Shadow Box: An Amateur in the Ring*. He observed later, with faux humility, 'I am not properly constituted to fight. I am built rather like a bird of the stilt-like, wader variety – the avocets, limpkins and herons. Since boyhood, my arms have remained stick-like. I can slide my watch up my arm almost to my elbow. I have a thin, somewhat fragile nose which bleeds easily.'

The addendum to this self-conscious put-down, of course, is that Plimpton wants us to appreciate his courage in the face of overwhelming odds. And rightly so, perhaps, but it serves no useful purpose beyond that of affording the writer a unique experience. As Gallico liked to tell people, he had received a minor public beating from the heavyweight champion of the world and thus had insinuated himself into a long and honourable lineage of real fighting men. It was always a tenuous claim. Drunks who took up John L Sullivan's challenge in bars around Boston and New York probably were closer to the real thing than any of these lettered gentlemen.

Miller, who resided in the same literary pond as Gallico and Plimpton, had similar ambitions for his book. And he writes beautifully of his experience. He claimed some expertise in martial arts – which, in the context of the event, was a bit like someone who has been in an aeroplane comparing himself with John Glenn. Ali said to him, with no hint of equivocation, 'Are you scared? Are you scared? Just think who you're with. How's it feel, knowin' you're in the ring with The Greatest of All Times?'

And how did it feel, Davis? In print, he rejoices in the tiniest success: '... rocketing a spinning backfist-left hook combination straight into the center of the right side of his jaw.' At this point, most amateur assailants – whatever the friendly pre-arrangement – would have left the ring, the room and possibly the country – quickly. Miller was trapped in the contract of his own making, though. To his credit, he took the inevitable retribution stoically. As if, given his boast of proficiency, he had any choice.

'I see the punch coming; it's a piece of red cinnamon and exactly the size of a gloved fist. I try to move away and can't – it's that fast. The back of my head bounces off of my shoulders. A chorus of white light goes off behind my eyes. There's a metal taste in my mouth, then a second, heavier thump. The spectators suddenly sound way, way off; my legs go to soup beneath me. He knows I'm hurt and he steps back. It's obvious he could knock me out with a single punch. I'm sure that most boxers would be pleased to do so. Instead, his eyes go kind, he slides an arm around my shoulders, we exchange hugs and smiles, and it's over.'

As a writing experience, it was a gift to Miller: a bit of pain, a buzzed brain for a few seconds – or maybe days – and the right to say, à la Gallico, that he'd put himself into that short line of human beings who'd traded some punches with the heavyweight champion of the world. Vain? Certainly. But it took courage, too. Miller at least deserves credit for that, however brief was his joust (he will look back on it as if it passed in a nanosecond). As a writer's view of the sheer heat, power and danger of the boxing life, it served some minor purpose, perhaps. But for Ali, as a preparation for what was to come against Frazier, it was not even the flexing of a little finger. And we should keep that in mind. There is a monumental gap between the actual and the perceived in boxing. Only a fighter, a real fighter, properly understands that. The rest of us are guessing at the size of the chasm. And we ought never doubt that Ali was a real fighter, however beautiful, smart and kind he was at the same time.

Most writers share Miller's undiluted love of Ali – but not all. Which brings us to our second example of the genre. Among the doubters is Jack Cashill – and he is worth listening to.

In 2006, Cashill wrote a book called *Sucker Punch*. Originally it was subtitled: *Ali, Islam and the Betrayal of the Dream*, which later was changed to: *The Hard Left Hook That Dazed and Killed King's Dream*. Both are clunking, neither is ambiguous. This book will return to Cashill later, but the gist of his thesis is that Ali has been the beneficiary of the (largely white and guilty) liberal left's unquestioning support for what he calls, 'the grievance narrative' that attends the history of African-Americans. As a white, blue-collar, hard-core native of New Jersey who grew up in the Clay/Ali era and appears to have drifted with some enthusiasm to the right, Cashill says he is qualified to offer an alternative view to that expounded by the overwhelming majority of writers on this fascinating man. He balances on a razor's edge for much of his book – not all of which is bunkum. But it is staggeringly partial, a determined effort of counter-intuitive writing, setting its face against the tidal wave of positivism that has enveloped Ali since his retirement, and, in so doing, he sometimes loses sight of the good while dwelling on the bad. Cashill goes in search of the negative, and he finds enough to satisfy his polemic. For some it is an uncomfortable read. But it should not be dismissed out of hand because it does serve one purpose and that is to take a look into some of the dark corners of Ali's life, and there have been a few.

Now, if you will indulge me, here is my take on Muhammad Ali.

Chapter One
Bicycle Thieves

If there is an enduring truth in professional boxing it is that theft speaks all languages. Prizefighters for centuries have been robbed of many things: money, dreams, dignity and, in the saddest circumstances, their lives. Fighting, embedded in Western culture through centuries of casual violence, became business in Georgian England when dissolute members of the aristocracy capitalised on that brutishness and laid aside their distaste of the underclasses long enough to make organised pugilism acceptable. Strengthening this contract between rich and poor was the uniquely British concept of muscular Christianity, where the devil met God. Those were the building blocks of boxing as a sport, mainly as a vehicle for gambling, with no regard for the welfare of its front-line participants.

What turned prizefighting from barbarism

conducted secretly in fields and on river barges into the commercial extravaganza it is today was the conviction of the moguls of the sports entertainment industry in the twentieth century that the desperation of brave and poor men offered limitless opportunities for them to make vast sums of money without risking personal injury to body or wallet. It was not a fair or just enterprise then, and it is not now. Nor, these rich men discovered, would it ever disappear. When that particular penny dropped – about the time the moving image began to enchant millions and sports stadiums started to bulge with massed voyeurs – the process was irreversible. In this evolution, no corner of society has been immune to boxing's charms. It has touched men and women, kings and vagabonds, scoundrels and adventurers, intellectuals and idiots. How could it die with a demographic as all-embracing as that? The fuel that drives the engine is, of course, money. Given that it survives on the thinnest moral premise and is as addictive as heroin, paid fist-fighting trails only war and the stock market as the ultimate expression of raw capitalism. The Hollywood utterance of capitalism's great anti-hero, Gordon Gekko, 'Greed is good', found a home in the boxing ring long before it hit Wall Street.

As with all forms of the greed industry, boxing does not discriminate on the grounds of sentiment or concern for others. Like war, it demands sacrifice from the weakest, with the spoils going to those who need it least. Like the stock market, it purports to give all of its soldiers a fighting chance, even if such a concept ignores its core truth: there are no winners without losers. Boxing is a contract of mutual exploitation, signed by all parties in the pursuit of hard cash masquerading as glory. To imagine otherwise is to surrender to shameless sentimentality. If you agree with that view, what follows might make some sense. If not, you are in the wrong part of the bookshop.

I have to admit to an unkillable, illogical love of boxing. There is a fair strain of it running through both sides of my family. And, while there is also ambiguity, doubts fade at the announcement of every major fight. Boxing has been the meat and drink of my professional life. I earn my living writing about men (and, lately, women) hitting each other in the head. Ultimately, against my better instincts and the advice of smart friends, I love boxing. But I am not sure I will ever truly understand it. Just as Ali accommodates Parkinson's disease, a lot of us come to a guilty understanding with the fight business.

When gathering my thoughts for this book – or, more likely, looking for a distraction while waiting for a single thought to come along – I flipped on a

DVD of *Bicycle Thieves*. It is a movie of searing simplicity about an ordinary man looking for work in late-1940s Italy, with the echoes and the dust of the Second World War settling still on recently vacated battlefields. On the face of it, *Bicycle Thieves* had nothing to do with boxing, yet it had much to do with survival, and those two things definitely are connected. Ricci, a man of meagre means, applies for a job in his small town and his prospective employer tells him he must have a bicycle to get the job. Ricci tells him that, yes, he does own a bicycle – then sets about getting one. He pawns his bedsheets, buys a bicycle and gets the job.

After this innocuous deception, Ricci finds himself in a minor role in the dream-selling business. His chores include sticking up posters of Rita Hayworth and contemporary American movie stars whose glamour illuminates the lives of the town's impoverished citizens via the local cinema. Ricci identifies with these famous strangers. He is, he tells himself, a member of their galaxy, not just a poor Italian scraping a living in post-war desolation. And he imagines his friends will be pleased and grateful to be so touched by this association. All of a sudden, he has invented another world for himself. And he hopes, too, that he can earn a little money. Ricci did not choose this as a career, however, it chose him.

For the film's creators, the Marxist writer Cesare Zavattini and the director Vittorio De Sica, the story is their critique of a political and moral system they mistrust. They contend that man's values are eternally compromised by circumstance: man will lie to live, and those of his comrades who are corrupted by the system will live to lie. In a sledgehammer metaphor, Zavattini and De Sica argue that the dilemma is cyclical, like the revolutions of a bicycle's wheel, turned again and again by helpless men passing their own burden on to others, all of them victims of oppression, but all of them manipulators too. In the inevitable twist to the tale, Ricci's bicycle is stolen by someone who is as desperate as he had been. He finds the thief (with ladled imagery, in a brothel, the quintessential palace of exploitation) but he cannot prove it is his bicycle. So he steals another one ... and the cycle, if you like, is repeated.

It is a near-perfect metaphor for the boxing industry.

In the summer of 1954, five years after *Bicycle Thieves* opened to critical acclaim in Europe, a person or persons unknown stole a young black boy's new $60 red Schwinn bicycle from outside the Columbia Auditorium in downtown Louisville, Kentucky. It was the site of an expo for black businessmen and, as free food was on offer, it was a magnet for young rascals not much interested in the grown-up concerns of commerce but familiar with the thrill of a complimentary hot dog. Among them was the young boy who had just had his bicycle stolen. Incensed by the theft, he complained to a police officer who was nearby supervising, as it happens, a team of young boxers. On the recommendation of Officer Joe Martin, the boy took up boxing, ostensibly to cultivate fighting skills with which to confront the thief. The tale has the ring of convenience about it, given what was to follow, but that is the version of the stolen bicycle as it has been handed down. Unlike Ricci, the boy did not find the miscreant; if he had, the script might have changed right there, with who knows what sort of ending. However, the boy did take up the officer's suggestion – and he did become quite brilliant at boxing. Six years after he lost his bicycle, Cassius Clay won an Olympic gold medal in the country that provided the setting for *Bicycle Thieves*. He already had a Roman name; now he had a Roman trinket.

In the post-war maelstrom of uncertainty and chaos, there were some inevitable contradictions. The Americans had conquered the Italians (with help from their Allies) and were then embraced by the vanquished, a tradition as old as the Roman Empire.

The American GIs, who not long before had been bombing them to bits, were now their saviours and heroes. And the culture from which they sprang was heroic also; you can't beat Hollywood.

True to this rolling narrative of disappointment, when Clay returned from the 1960 Rome Olympics hailed as an American hero – like the soldiers twenty-five years before him had been when they came back from conquering and seducing Europe – he was reminded that he was still regarded as a second-class citizen in the divided South. Cassius, a young black sporting hero in a white-ruled society, was every bit as powerless a victim of 'the system' as was Ricci. It is said he was so angered by the hypocrisy of a community who hailed his victory yet despised his presence that he threw his Olympic gold medal into the Ohio River. By this point, however, he was caught up in another cycle of theft: the sport and business of professional boxing. What he could not have suspected then was that he would become the most celebrated athlete in the world, and much more – but, nevertheless, 'still a nigga' as he is inclined to remind people to this day.

These were the formative episodes in the life of Muhammad Ali, as Cassius Clay became. They were the early chapters of one of the great stories of twentieth-century sport, about an athlete who transcended his discipline and the business of the fight industry. And they are so deeply planted in the public imagination as to invite charges of heresy if questioned. Are they true? Did someone really steal young Cassius's bike? Did the Olympic champion really throw his gold medal into the Ohio River?

For his part, Davis Miller got what seemed to be a great scoop when he resumed his relationship with Ali in 1989. In a telephone conversation, Miller is telling Ali about how he has sold a story he wrote, called 'My Dinner With Ali', to a sports magazine, and they want photos to go with it, but just of his hands. Ali is sceptical – or sounds like he is. On pages 204–5, Miller writes:

"'You ain't no writer,' he says, when I get up the nerve to tell him why I've called. "They just usin' you."

"I've wanted to write for years. Like you, when you threw your gold medal off the bridge, I threw my beeper in the river and quit my job so I could write."

"I never did that," he says.

"Did what?" I ask.

"Never threw my medal off no bridge. Just lost it, that's all."

"You serious?"

"Mmmmm, that's a story I made up. I know what it takes to sell a story."

"What matters," I say, "is the way you influenced me. What matters is I did it because I thought you had.'"

So, who to believe, what to believe. Ultimately, it depends on whichever definition of the truth you find most convenient. Ali, a prisoner of his own invention, was as keen to believe in the tricks and stunts he performed throughout his career as were the mesmerised members of his audience – such as Miller – a constituency that would be numbered in several millions. It suited everyone to believe some of the outrageous things he said and did because to pretend otherwise would be to kill the magic. If you forgave him his enthusiasm for major and minor manipulation of the facts, yes, these tales were, in the very widest sense of the word, true. They were true for those who wanted to believe. For Ali, that was good enough. In an industry built on lies, Ali was as honest as any other trickster.

It is helpful to accept a loose interpretation of what constitutes truth in the fight game to properly understand Ali. Not only was he drawn to invention and inconsequential mischief, his life and his sport are littered with lies and half-truths, innocent and profound. He was romanced (with little resistance) by people who recognised him as the ultimate salesman for whatever it was they were selling, from tickets to a boxing match to religion and politics and, in the sad end, to scraps of his glorious past reheated in the auction houses of the world as boxing memorabilia.

As I was finishing this book, in July 2014, the gloves Ali wore in the Fight of the Century, his first meeting with Joe Frazier, at Madison Square Garden in 1971 when both men were unbeaten, were listed for sale at an auction in Cleveland. This was not unusual – except this was the second time in two years the gloves had been sold. Their lineage was interesting. The first time they were sold, they came from the estate of Ali's career-long trainer and friend, Angelo Dundee, who plainly had received them as a gift from his fighter. Dundee died in February 2012. In December that year, his son, Jim, sold them for $385,848 to help pay medical bills. At the same auction, for the same price, a collector also picked up the gloves Ali wore when he beat Sonny Liston in 1964 to win the world heavyweight title for the first time. There is more to this recycling story: in February 2014, near the first fight's fiftieth anniversary, the Ali-Liston gloves were sold for a second time, this time bringing $836,500, more than 200 per cent profit in less than two years. What would the Fight of the Century gloves return their lucky owner in July 2014? An anonymous bidder paid $388,375, less than half that paid for the gloves from the first Liston fight. Memories fade, even those of Ali. 'These gloves are more than sports memorabilia,' said the auction's organiser, Chris Ivy. 'They're artefacts of early 1970s American pop culture.'

And there's me thinking there was no distinction between sports memorabilia and 'artefacts of … pop culture' which go on sale for nearly half a million pounds. Whatever you like to call them (battered old boxing gloves?), I bet they made someone other than the original owner a good deal richer.

Here's the oddity, though: Ali would not care. He has probably given away millions of dollars worth of tat during and after his career. It is not that he does not know his own worth – when he came to London in 1999, for example, to be celebrated as the greatest athlete of the twentieth century, it cost the organisers $100,000 – even though Ali long ago ceased caring about material things. He is comfortable. He lives modestly. What money comes his way as the most marketable living relic of the past century goes to his eponymous foundation in Louisville, which does much good work in the community and beyond. It is not the passing on of the gloves that matters, however. They are only gloves. They could be left in the corner of any old gym, picked up and treasured for ever more. No, it is the commerce they generate, the profit that one party makes from a fighter's working tools, the gloves that guard the knuckles that crack the skulls of his opponents for our enjoyment. It is an odd business, altogether.

Perhaps the most bizarre example of this curious trade was the case of the cigarette paper. In 1961, the renowned boxing historian and memorabilia – sorry, artefacts – collector Hank Kaplan met a young Cassius Clay in Dundee's 5th Street Gym in Miami. Clay, the most engaging and involved of individuals, paused after his workout and noticed Kaplan smoking a cigarette. According to legend, he took the cigarette from his hand and, in a delicate hand, signed it. Many years later, that cigarette paper went for $1,900 at auction – just as Clay knew it would.

So, there have been many people – not just managers and promoters – who have co-opted Ali's words, achievements and property for their own ends, interpreting them to suit, or selling them on. You could say this book is an example of that. You could say that I am no better or worse than Dundee, Kaplan or any of the others who trawl Ali's life and go to work on it; and you could be right. But I will try to keep it as honest as I know how. Not everything is as it seems, though.

Ali's personality perfectly suited his accidental calling because he was a born kidder, and an illusionist who retained a life-long fascination with simple magic tricks, who loved to joke and mess around, forever deriving pleasure from harmless japes. In the ring, such an inclination can bring success and it can bring pain. Ali and boxing were the perfect partners – even if, like Ricci, he did not choose boxing. Boxing chose him.

At the heart of the sport of boxing (as distinct from the business) is an understanding between fighters that requires them to indulge in an unspoken dialogue during the course of a bout. It goes something like this: you must believe you are better than your opponent, even if you suspect you are not; you must persuade first yourself and then your opponent of your conviction, no matter the legitimacy or otherwise of the evidence. He, similarly, will tell himself and you the same lie, and you will either believe him or you will consider him fraudulent. When it is done, the fighter who has created the most convincing narrative and played it out to the satisfaction of hopefully independent arbiters, exposing the other man as the least believable liar, will be declared the winner. That is how boxing works: you reach the unavoidable truth through an elaborate confection of half-truths. Ali's ability to deceive sustained a boxing career in which he held a spell over nearly all of his opponents. Few who came into contact with him – inside or outside the ring – wanted to or were able to resist his charms. Hypnotised, they were desperate to believe what he had to say. For all but five of his sixty-one opponents, such surrender to his will led to inevitable defeat.

For all that he mesmerised fighters, fans and the media, however, Ali was real. He actually was what he said he was: The Greatest. He beat them all. He delivered on his magic trick time and again. He wrote poems predicting exactly what he would do, and, for a briefly wondrous time, he did not disappoint. Thomas Hauser, one of his biographers, estimates he got the round right the first twelve times he made a prediction. And then he stopped. Whatever the number, he confounded all the anointed experts (especially those more potent with a pen than a glove) who proclaimed he did too many things wrong in the ring. Men such as Norman Mailer, who asserted with the certainty only an egotist could muster that Ali did not conform to any known orthodoxy from the time-dusted book of boxing wisdom. Sitting ringside in Kinshasa, Zaire, at the Rumble in the Jungle in 1974 with George Plimpton, another American intellectual hooked on the glamour of the fight game, Mailer gave Ali no chance against George Foreman. Plimpton agreed. They were not necessarily wrong because of their rudimentary boxing analysis (nearly all the hard-core boxing types agreed with them) but because, for once, they and everyone else stopped believing in a phenomenon they had helped create. Within eight rounds, Ali made fools of all the wise men. He did not care what they said because, underneath his megaphone boasts, he knew he was blessed and he placed absolute faith in his God-given talent, as well as his own brand of magic. 'Ali Bomaye!' the crowd chanted in Lingala: 'Ali, kill him!' He didn't do that, but he knocked Foreman out. Then they believed; all of them. Some rewrote their sentiments. 'Oh my God, he's won the title back at thirty-two!' Harry Carpenter famously shouted into his BBC microphone. But they were all back in the Ali business, beneficiaries of a boxing miracle conjured by the sport's great magician.

There were so many nights like this. For believers – like fans of Roger Federer who will not listen to cynics who insist he can never regain the dominance that brought him seventeen grand slam titles – it is no more than what they expect to happen. They have faith. When Ali's gifts began to properly dissipate, however, there could be no avoiding the cruel full stop to the first chapter of his life. It arrived on 11 December 1981, in the Queen Elizabeth Stadium in Nassau, the Babylonian capital of the tax haven of the Bahamas. This was a place where lying was legitimised and rewarded. It was twenty-seven years after young Cassius's bike was stolen. There were no nuanced exchanges, no pretence or fooling around, no rabbits left in the hat, just a lot of public suffering and humiliation. It was a Friday and, for what remained of Ali as a professional fighter, not a very good Friday. For half an hour, the hollow clack of a cowbell (requisitioned at the last minute from a nearby field, so tawdry was the promotion) interrupted the three-minute beatings, spread over ten rounds, which a strong young Canadian called Trevor Berbick administered on the shell of a once-magnificent athlete. Ali, a giant in our lives for two decades and more, shrank towards invisibility in the space of half an hour in front of a smattering of bemused locals and cynical insiders. It was an ignominious end, a sad, lonely conclusion to the most wonderful adventure any of us had been privileged to celebrate.

That Sunday in the *Observer*, Hugh McIlvanney wrote that witnessing Ali lose for the fifth and final time was like watching, 'a prince leave town on the back of a dust cart'.

While Ali's story would not differ in many respects from those of most prizefighters – boxing encourages extravagant swings in fortune – it was unique. He was, indeed, that prince – a prince like no other. He would get down off the dust cart, put his crown shakily back on his handsome head and deal us several decades more of his peculiar entertainment, much of it silent, all of it poignant, none of it dull.

There is no other fighter who so convincingly has extended his story beyond the final punch, or could even have dreamt of doing so. Some tried: Gene Tunney, the heavyweight champion from the 1920s and a friend of George Bernard Shaw, fancied himself as something of a writer and thinker, but was never taken seriously, so laboured were his literary efforts after he retired; Sugar Ray Robinson, an extrovert from the same entertainment ballpark as Ali, who travelled with an entourage of personal barbers, circus midgets and sycophants, took his dancing feet to the stage, but failed to reproduce the level of brilliance he achieved in the ring with those same educated feet, and he died in a haze of dementia; poor Joe Frazier, unfairly taunted by Ali all his career, could not make much headway in a brief diversion as a singer, and was destined to be the minor player in his rival's drama, all the way to his grave; Archie Moore, the Ol' Mongoose, a fighter whose longevity straddled the Second World War (he famously lost to an emerging Cassius Clay, then very briefly trained him), also had a touch of showmanship, talking in his post-fighting days as if he were an ennobled Englishman. Yet Archie too was in Ali's shadow. None of these made the wider impact that Ali did or in the manner that he did it, with a mere half-smile sometimes, or a cheek-filled rant, mugging up for any camera that came into view. None of his fellow fighting brothers matched him for reach, as modern-day brand marketers put it. Nobody was as funny, mischievous or just plain crazy.

There is no one Muhammad Ali, however. Just as there was no one Cassius Clay, the chrysalis from whom Ali emerged. In the following pages, I will look for some of them. The search should be illuminating. Along the way we might understand how this perplexing individual, a man with probably as many flaws as virtues, persuaded us to believe in him. It might have been because he held up a mirror to our own inadequacies and the flickering heroism to which even the most humble individual aspires. It could just have been that we found him endlessly entertaining and pretended the fascination had stronger roots. Or it possibly was all of that and more.

While this is not just a book about boxing and a boxer's ring exploits, there will be a smattering of left hooks and knockouts, because that was the meat of his trade. But I hope I can tell the equally interesting story of Muhammad Ali: the man with two names who happened to be a boxer. If he had not boxed, he would have been outrageous in some other way, of that there is little question. Nobody that loud would remain unheard for long. But he ended up in the right job, by the happiest of accidents. Once he found it, Ali knew he was as made for boxing as was a glove. The fit was perfect in every way. Just as Fred Astaire, surely, was born to dance, or Frank Sinatra destined to sing, so Ali had to be a fighter. Even though he was not by nature violent, he had 'fight' in him, the unquantifiable gene. He had a stage on which to perform, 20ft by 20ft, a white canvas lit brightly in a darkened room and which, at the end of the performance, was left bloodied by the efforts of the actors. Ali used that canvas to paint moving pictures every bit as powerful as any that Martin Scorsese could conjure on the big screen.

Like many boxers, he embraced a sport for which he had shown no predisposition until circumstance intervened, and that is a fascinating comma in the story. How and why did Ali become a boxer?

Whatever the truth of the bicycle story, he did meet Joe Martin and Martin did encourage him to box. What happened after that seems inevitable, in retrospect, because of the young man's natural talent. But it might not have turned out that way. There is a theory – well argued by Frans Johansson in *The Click Moment: Seizing Opportunity in an Unpredictable World* – that suggests there is no such thing as luck, just millions of streams of converging incidents. Johansson writes: 'When Richard Williams heard in 1980 that Romanian tennis player Virginia Ruzici earned $40,000 in one day for winning a minor tournament, something inside him clicked. He turned to his wife and said: "Let's have more kids and make them tennis players." Venus Williams was born in June of that year, followed by Serena in 1981.' You know the rest. Or, as Bob Dylan sang, 'Think what you have gathered from coincidence.'

So, what if Ali had not gone to town on his new bicycle that October day in 1954? What if he had not found boxing? Would he have left his mark? It is impossible to say, of course. He might have followed his father into the sign-writing business, although he showed no aptitude for that. (Certainly, he was a lousy poet.) Perhaps he would have been a preacher. He had an obvious oratorical bent, and he came from a Baptist tradition that encouraged such expression. He was undoubtedly funny enough to be a professional comedian – many say that is exactly what he was: a one-man Punch and Judy show, the master puppeteer of our emotions. He might have fulfilled the stereotyped prophesy of a career in crime, the ultimate insult to his race. It is not patronising to say, however, he probably was not destined for a career in nuclear physics, given the United States government initially failed him on his army entrance exam, and his own admission that he found reading and the other trappings of considered thought a burden. His wit was verbal, and he relayed all of his innate intelligence with chilling efficiency on to the chins of his opponents through his educated fists.

What we can reasonably assume is that he would not have been mediocre. Ali once echoed McIlvanney's dustcart metaphor when asked what might have become of him had he not been heavyweight champion of the world. 'I would have been the world's greatest at whatever I did,' he said. 'If I were a garbage man, I'd be the world's greatest garbage man! I'd pick up more garbage and faster than anyone has ever seen. To tell you the truth, I would have been the greatest at whatever I'd done!'

And he would have been. At least he would have believed that to be the case ... and so, more than likely, would we.

Ali's deeds have been set down in more than fifty books, countless documentaries and a couple of films, testimony to the grip he holds on not only the public but the industry that feeds a universal fascination for legal violence. I have read and liked many of the books, seen the films and documentaries, and I trust that has not sluiced my thinking too much, because a lot of myth has been grafted on to his story. Maybe there is more to come, good and bad, true and unimaginably not.

Alone among modern fighters, certainly, Ali rose above his calling. He revelled in the artistry of boxing. It was the perfect medium in which to express sentiments that had very little to do with the sport and business of boxing. The ring was his stage and the microphone they put in front of him after each performance the next link to his public. Even he was as enthused by his own rhetoric as others were and he often let the words flow like punches. He was also led by others, people who seized on his unique power to cajole and convince, to push an idea, no matter what the idea was. They used him – and they used him up. Shamelessly.

However, over time, the purpose of his journey

began to crystallise in front of his widening eyes. Even before his first coronation as the king of boxing, when he whipped Sonny Liston in Miami in 1964, just like he said he would, he was morphing from Cassius Clay into Muhammad Ali. The transformation would alienate him. It scared a constituency of knuckle-scraping sadists who wanted nothing more complicated than to see a man laid horizontal in a boxing ring and were not concerned with his religion, his politics or the theatrical pronouncements of a wired-up young champion. They hated him, in fact. Not in the same way they hated the gangster's pawn Liston, or for the same reasons. But they did hate him, whatever the revisionism that was layered on the story afterwards. Anyone who grew up in his time will have no problem recalling the hostility directed towards Ali when he would not shut up, when he refused to 'know his place'. The term 'uppity nigger' is a horrible one, and horrible people applied it to Ali with glee.

How this mere pugilist with the big mouth and sharp brain would go on to make these same haters love him – indeed to make most of the planet fall for him without reservation – is as much a triumph of his personality as a conundrum. They did not gather at the hem of his cloak because he was a messiah (as he sometimes might have imagined, because disciples and manipulators told him it was so). They cared little for the substance of what he had to say about the tenets of Islam or, more particularly, that off-shoot version of it he once supported; nor were they universally convinced he was right about his objections to fighting in Vietnam, although plenty said they agreed with him, partly because it suited the mood of America in a time of ferment; they should have been offended by his sexist and racist remarks, but they set aside those reservations.

More members of the entranced audience should have been appalled at how he belittled Joe Frazier, too, but Ali was the 'great convincer'. He could get away with just about anything. Once he had hypnotised his followers, he could do no wrong. They listened, rapt, to the music of his words and paid good money to hear him talk and see him fight because he was a near-perfect invention, an entertainer and athlete who could talk and perform, sometimes simultaneously. He married the two skills perfectly. When the young Ali said he would knock out his opponent in a certain round and then did so, it was as if he had pulled off the most amazing magic trick. And even when the old Ali stopped making predictions and was happy to survive against younger, stronger opponents trying to tear his head off, his audience trusted him still. They willed him to win, because he was part of their own past. To abandon him would be an act of betrayal, as well as an admission of their own gullibility. Even with the help of distance, some members of the vast entourage refused to take another look. It is their loss. They are missing the whole picture.

Ali did something else, though. As much as he seduced them as customers at the gate, he took their lust for gore and turned it into the polar opposite: love. I doubt this was his original purpose; like Dylan when he arrived in New York with his guitar and his talent – long before he became profound and wise – all he ever wanted was a hit to make some money. But another imperative was at work inside Ali's complex mind: he found himself, inadvertently, on a journey of self-discovery. As he went down that road, falling among thieves and hucksters, he learnt. It took him quite a while. Way too long for his own good, say those closest to him now. When the light went on, it was too late to save his boxing career, but the revelations that bathed him made Ali a new man. No longer could he shout, because he had been gripped by Parkinson's disease, but he did not need to. He was eloquent in his palsied silence. He exuded a strange calm. The fighting had stopped and the peace had begun. Nostalgics craved the showman, but he was never coming back once his brain had started to slowly accommodate the damage accumulated over nearly three decades of fighting. He resided now in another land, still smiling knowingly, still laughing quietly, at himself and others. But he was wiser now, content despite the concern of those who cared about him. Finally he had settled on some honest reflections. People who had cheered him in the ring when he was young, pretty and so very much alive, now smiled in appreciation of a quietened man to whom they had a lifetime connection. We were all part of the same morality play, in a way. There was no reason – or evidence – to assume Ali had become a saint; but he no longer had the energy or will to be a devil.

There is not a person I know who has been in Ali's presence who does not in some way feel a form of love towards him. Women, still, are entranced by his obvious (and scurrilous) charm; men are drawn to his cheek, humour and masculine bravado, once a comic turn with a punch to garnish the laughs, and now a respected retiree. But the affection that speaks loudest is that which carries no baggage and has no agenda, nothing to sell. Nobody understands Ali like children do. He speaks to them without words, and the conversation is mutually satisfying. They share with him the naivety we all once knew, even if most of us threw it away. This is fascinating, because these children can never have known the other Ali, the loud one, the one who knocked out grown men, the great boxing magician. They only knew this version of Ali, the permanently mute one, the one who communicates now by the force of his inner peace. Children rely more on gut feeling than learnt response, so their sentiments are not corrupted by outside prejudices or the judgments of others. That is what Ali tapped into with children, a pure honesty. And they recognised it in him, instantly, this uncorrupted love. Ali, who had survived many cruelties and perpetrated a few himself, never shed his childish ways. He kept the smile in his eyes. Nobody found that damn bike, by the way. Nor the gold medal ...

Chapter Two
Veni, Vidi, Vici

We take much for granted in the age of instant communication. Telling the world (or our bit of it) what we have just had for breakfast is a few smartphone strokes away on Twitter. Knowledge is on tap, instantly, through a bewildering array of gadgets. From the top of a mountain in Africa to a barrio in Rio, information flies through the ether without impediment or reflection. It is an enduring paradox that the more science makes our lives easier, the more our existence becomes complicated, more intense. These instruments of freedom imprison us in their iron grip, making us as dependent on something as innocent as a mobile phone, as a crackhead is on their dealer.

The evolution of communication in 1960 had not reached such a frenzied state. Fame lasted longer than fifteen minutes, whatever Andy Warhol said.

Life was simple: not in the way it might be meant today – as in stripped of inconvenience or drudgery – but properly simple, pared down, easy to understand. People wrote letters to each other, and sent postcards. Making a telephone call might require a knock on a neighbour's door, asking to use their heavy, plastic gadget.

Cassius Clay was a child of the information revolution, and would become one of its most verbose stars. But when he left the United States for the first time, as a member of the 1960 US Olympic boxing team competing in the XXVII Olympiad in Rome, a lithe and innocent light-heavyweight from Louisville, young Cassius was as unaware as the rest of us of the tumult he was about to create. Indeed, this brave fighter who was petrified of flying nearly refused to go. As Joe Martin's son told the Louisville *Courier-Journal*, 'He finally agreed to fly. But then he went to an army surplus store and bought a parachute and actually wore it on the plane. It was a pretty rough flight. He was now in the aisle, praying with his parachute on.' Once he got to Rome and did what he did, he still had no idea of the fuss and bother and excitement he would bring to our lives. The ignorance would not last long.

The 1960 Rome Olympics were the first to be shown on television in North America, although getting the pictures into those households was not as straightforward as it would subsequently become. Satellite broadcasts were still two years away so CBS, which had the TV rights in the United States, joined with its partners, CBC of Canada and Mexico's Televisa, in rushing videotape from the venues to editing suites in the city, from where they were transferred to Paris to be tidied up and put on to new tapes and flown by jet to Idlewild Airport (later renamed JFK) in New York. From there, mobile units fed the tapes to the offices of CBS, CBC and Televisa. Sometimes, viewers saw the events on the day they took place.

What they saw when they turned on their black-and-white television sets – standing on stiff, thin plastic legs in the corners of their living rooms – to watch the boxing was the most engaging sight. There in the Palazzo dello Sport – in a complex built in the southern suburbs of Rome in 1932 to celebrate the Fascist architecture so beloved of Benito Mussolini – a princely figure, gleaming in youthful health, danced for their entertainment. It was in the same arena that the US won their fifth straight Olympic basketball gold medal, and the team's stars, including Jerry West, Walt Bellamy and Jerry Lucas, all destined for their sport's Hall of Fame, were considerably more prominent on the public radar at the time than the loud young Kentuckian. That would soon change. Cassius Clay was to take hold of the medium that showcased his outrageous talent and used it as if it were his personal property. No athlete, before or since, so captured the spotlight trained on him and worked it to his own requirements and whims. Like Marilyn Monroe and Elvis Presley, he was born for the camera. In Rome, his American teammates called him, 'the Mayor of the Olympic Village', as he went from team to team, country to country, trading Olympic lapel pins and telling anyone who would listen how good he was and what he was going to do to his opponents. Already he was developing a taste for public performance. And he would flower in front of a microphone, not at all nervous performing for interviewers with egos that almost matched his own, most famously the wig-topped Howard Cosell, with whom he would form a partnership as popular as the one between Dean Martin and Jerry Lewis in that era.

But it was in the boxing ring where the fighter's eloquence was unavoidable. You could almost hear him box. His was a gift of movement granted to few. He weighed a little under fourteen stone at the time, was as light on his feet as the gravity-defying Russian ballet dancer Rudolf Nureyev, as quick as a middleweight and as potent as most operators in the heavyweight division above him. It was not the weight of his punch that made him dangerous, because he was more of a whiplash artist than a pounding bully, but his speed. If you could capture it in your vision in an age when slow motion replays were a luxury, you were doing well. His gloves blurred the TV screen that projected images in blurry detail and his opponents had about as much chance of calculating their arc and point of impact as did the viewers. The blows came from all angles and at no pre-determined moment. He was a natural. Nobody taught him to punch with both feet off the ground, or while moving backwards in a straight line towards the ropes while his prey advanced witlessly into range. Nobody recommended in those more structured times that a boxer present his chin as a present, only to withdraw it at the last possible moment and punish its pursuer with a rasping whack.

Amateur boxing was different then. There was a considerable scoring emphasis on skill and it was considered as artful to make an opponent miss as it was to land a blow. When the young American moved, then, it was with the quickly gathered understanding of the sport's abiding mantra: hit and don't be hit; be first, too, if you can; throw in bunches; do not let your elbow stray behind the invisible line of your ribs; hook off the jab; finish with a hook; move to your left against a compulsive hooker; hook around a southpaw's leading right jab; do not get square on; bend your knees; punch from the balls of your feet; punch through the target.

Ali knew all of these mantras, listened to some, ignored many of them and just did his thing. He did not stick slavishly to rules or instructions. He went where his heart and his feet took him and it was invariably to a place of his choosing, where older, more orthodox opponents reckoned they might be able to exploit his eccentric habits, only to find that he could spring at them like a cat in the dark, then leave just as quickly, giving them little more than fresh air to fight. This was the sort of boxing that Sugar Ray Robinson boxed. This was the sort of boxing Benny Leonard, Willie Pep and other eccentric talents employed. This was the sort of boxing that Howard Cosell could not understand in a month of Sundays.

There were no headguards then in amateur boxing, either – so people could actually see what the fighters looked like. This was doubly helpful for Clay. Not only did he establish a rapport with the audience, ringside and in the growing medium of television – which was spreading speedily beyond its local constituencies – but he could engage in eye contact with his opponent. And this is where he so often began to weave his spell. Boxers, amateur and professional, were not encouraged in those days to do anything else once the bell rang but stick to the script, stay disciplined behind a good jab, be brave, respect the referee and, under no circumstances, communicate with the other fighter by any other method than clocking him on the snout as hard as possible. Such constrictions never applied to Clay. From the beginning he rode his luck. He would taunt and jabber, eyes on fire, feet moving more like Astaire than Marciano. If he sensed a weakness, he would exploit it, not because he was necessarily cruel (not, at least, in the early days) but because he recognised it made sense. And what he found from the start was that because other boxers had no inclination to indulge themselves in such shenanigans, he had this whole theatrical field to himself. He was a one-man travelling circus, an act, a part of show business, a fighter destined for far greater things than winning a mere Olympic gold medal in the Palazzo dello Sport.

That, nevertheless, was where he launched his career. In his opening bout of the boxing tournament at the Rome Olympics, having received a first-round bye, Clay, entrant No 272, according to the number on the back of his white vest, was matched with a balding Belgian called Yvon Becot. Clay was eighteen, fresh-faced and weighed 176 lbs. Becot was twenty-four, a gnarled campaigner and a couple of pounds heavier. He was Belgium's best amateur light-heavyweight in the late 1950s, which is as damning with faint praise as it sounds. Clay took less than two rounds to bamboozle an honest but utterly outclassed athlete destined to be remembered outside his own country for little else but providing this amazing fighter with a home for a left hook which landed in the second round as if guided by God. Clay then whirred those dancing feet in what was to become known as the 'Ali Shuffle', and buzzed poor Becot for another minute. The Belgian was so disorientated after the referee's kind intervention that he was barely aware the fight had ended. He never spoke to his famous conqueror, but in later years he treasured the mauling. Becot had set young Cassius on his way.

So how was his entry to world sport presented? A handful of American journalists, in on the skinny, had been alerted to the arrival of their cocky compatriot and there was a frisson of interest, but no real belief that Clay was provably special. For the most part, newspapers, still overwhelmingly the main conduit for news in 1960, would stay with old values and judgments. This is how United Press International went out on the ticker to report

Clay's arrival in the wider consciousness of client newspapers. (Becot would not benefit from a checking of how his name was spelt.)

'Eighteen-year-old Cassius Clay, a lanky 6′2″ Negro from the United States competing in the [81kg] Light-Heavyweight Division exhibited lightning speed with sharp right-hand leads to score a 2nd-Round Referee Stoppage over Belgium's Yvon Becaus. The 30-year-old Belgian, a strong and aggressive fighter, could not match the speed of Clay late in Round 2, and was dropped by a quick left hook and smashing right to the chin. Becaus returned to fighting after receiving the Mandatory-Count, but was stunned again moments later when the "whippet thin" Clay caught him with hard chopping right to the side of the head, where the Referee issued a "safe" Standing 8-Count. The Referee permitted the bout to continue, and the Belgian tried to fight back, but was met with a fast double "left-right" to chin by Clay which rocked him backwards. The Referee stepped in to stop the action at 2:45 of Round 2 with Becaus still on his feet, but dazed from the onslaught from the American.'

It is not Damon Runyon, certainly, and it was more than likely knocked out in double-quick time from a telephone to copy-takers as literate in boxing as they were in moon landings, but it captures a flavour of the times and the moment, most strikingly in the reference to the 'lanky 6′2″ Negro', a description considered acceptable in the 1960s. That lanky youth would go on to return such passing laziness back on to the perpetrators over the years. As for Becot, it is said he had a brief and spectacularly unsuccessful professional career, boxing as Yvon Because. Why? Just Because. His place in boxing had been secured, even if his name had not.

After Mr Because came a string of Mr Why Did I Bothers? The one who was the last to taste Clay's punch for free was the very accomplished Pole Zbigniew Pietrzykowski, who is as bamboozled as he is bewitched by Clay, honoured in later years to say he shared a ring with the man who would become Muhammad Ali.

Chapter Three
Homecoming

These then were the early words of a story that grew before our unbelieving eyes. Clay won the gold medal in Rome and, like fighters before him, attempted the alchemy of turning the representation of wealth into the actual hard stuff. It is likely (although difficult to prove) that the Olympic final was watched by millions, or at least hundreds of thousands. But the significance of the achievement would soon be drowned in the myth that followed. It is worth briefly examining the circumstances leading up to the moment in which Clay is said to have flung his Olympic gold medal into the Ohio River on his return from Rome to Louisville.

In *The Greatest, My Own Story*, Ali, with the help of his unquestioning ghost writer, Richard Durham, describes the days and months after his homecoming, and how they bred confusion and disillusion. Clay knew from the moment he stepped down from the podium in Rome that he was going to turn professional and he wanted as his manager Joe Louis, boxing's finest heavyweight to that point (and still so, in the opinion of many), the paragon of the black sporting world, heir to the great Hitler-defying Olympian Jesse Owens. But Louis, who'd had a rough ride after his career had ended, was not keen. It was just as well. He'd endured a contractual mauling by the Mob at the end of his illustrious career, the taxman then ate into his funds, he gambled too freely on the golf course and he began to lose his grip on reality. Joe Louis in his fading years was testament to everything that is wrong about the fight game, and the sight of him shaking hands with punters as a greeter at Caesar's Palace in Las Vegas is among the saddest of my experience.

'Then I wanted Sugar Ray Robinson,' Ali wrote. But the second black God of boxing – who was still fighting – told him, 'Come back maybe in a couple of years, okay?' And Robinson, also, had problems. His memory was failing on him. He'd fought on for way too long and his judgment was not sharp enough now to deal with the sharks of the industry. Clay might not have appreciated any of this at the time, but either of those two black heroes would have been wrong for him at the outset of his professional career.

This was not what Clay expected, however. He wanted to be feted. He had a gold medal; he was destined for greatness. Why would the two greatest black boxers before him not want to help him achieve that? Was it jealousy? Maybe they were protecting their own legacy, he imagined. Or, more likely, they just did not recognise how great this young fighter was going to become.

Clay wanted to reach out to someone in his own community to guide his career. He was not immediately drawn to the Establishment for help. But Louis and Robinson were no revolutionaries. Robinson even had his own TV show. Indeed, like his namesake, Jackie Robinson, the first black man to play Major League baseball, Ray had happily been co-opted, to use the euphemism of the day, as an accepted member of the white mainstream entertainment industry. While Jackie Robinson had broken the race barrier in baseball, he was also innately conservative and patriotic. So was Louis. So was Sugar Ray. They were of the previous era.

But neither, at the time, was young Clay a firebrand storming the ramparts. His very name invited thoughts of moulding and, in 1960, he remained a work of art yet to be refined. Had white society seen fit, he would have been co-opted too. But Clay was different. He had a spark in him that reached back way beyond Robinson and Louis, all the way to the terrible rebel, Jack Johnson.

Jack Johnson was the real revolutionary. He was the fighter who changed boxing. He changed a significant part of American society too, although none of this was his mission. Johnson just wanted to do his thing – and that thing was to fight, fuck as many women as possible – white or black – and have a great time. Yet, through the force of his rebellious personality and the power in his clever fists, Johnson did change things. His is a remarkable story, one that Clay (or rather Ali) would come to appreciate in detail half a century and more later.

Johnson, famously – or infamously, in the eyes of white America – was the first black heavyweight champion of the world, feared and reviled in equal measure. Until Sonny Liston, he was also 'the baddest'. He set the bar high in notoriety and, although he did not intend to, Clay, as Ali, would raise it even further.

At the outset of his career, however, Clay was yet to find his political feet. But he did let his personality drive his growth, let his big young mouth do the talking. And he had plenty of black pride, which is why he reached out to Joe Louis and then Sugar Ray, the black heroes of his sport. Their rejection of him was to have consequences.

In his authorised autobiography, compiled in 1975 and stamped approvingly by the Nation of Islam, which he joined when he was eighteen, Ali reflects on Robinson's off-handedness with the sort of informed hindsight that characterises much of his subsequent thinking. 'I respected Sugar Ray in the ring as one of the greatest of all times. But he stayed out of what I call the real fighting ring, the one where freedom for black people in America takes place, and maybe if he had become my manager he might have influenced me to go his way. I'm glad he had no time.'

So where did young Clay, still to be revolutionised, take his gifts to be managed? To twelve white businessmen in Louisville – a city not named for Joe Louis, obviously, but for King Louis XVI of France. It was the genteel southern capital of old colonial values, a place for conformity and tradition among the refined godfathers of the thoroughbred horse-racing industry, whose cultural centrepiece was the Kentucky Derby, whose drink was Bourbon and whose face was white.

When Clay got off the plane from Rome, he was met in New York by Joe Martin, the cop who taught him to box and now envisaged a new career with the golden champion, and a Louisville millionaire called William Reynolds, who'd built his fortune in pots and pans, and lived behind a big iron gate on an estate in Bridgeton, one of Louisville's elite whites-only suburbs. Ali would later describe Martin as Reynolds's 'personal Man Friday' but, at the time, all of this courting by members of the white Establishment was perfectly acceptable for young Clay. Like Dylan and Presley, he just wanted his hit record.

The first bed Clay slept in after coming home was in a private suite Reynolds had set aside at New York's Waldorf Astoria hotel. Reynolds took Clay's parents – his father, Cash, and his mother, Bird – shopping in Manhattan. He told Clay when they sat down in a fancy restaurant, 'Eat all the steaks you can.' Cassius had six. He was still very much the innocent abroad – even when at home – the Clay waiting to be moulded.

When he got back to Louisville, they gave him a parade. Cash put up the red, white and blue on the porch of their humble house. The new champ had been away for twenty-one days, the longest trip of his life. Central High put out signs, 'WELCOME HOME CASSIUS CLAY'. The mayor gave him the keys to the city. Newspapers across Kentucky even said nice, patronising things about the young black boxer.

He even wrote a poem to mark the occasion:

To make America the greatest is my goal
So I beat the Russian and I beat the Pole
And for the USA won the medal of gold
The Greeks said you're better than the Cassius of old.

Like much of what was to follow, it didn't scan terribly well, but it dripped innocent pride. How could anyone not warm to this young ingénue?

'I was deeply proud of having represented America on a world stage,' Clay wrote in his book. 'To me, the gold medal was more than a symbol of what I had achieved for myself and my country; there was something I expected the medal to achieve for me. And, during those first days of homecoming, it seemed to be doing exactly that.'

Joe Martin made it clear to young Clay he wanted to be his manager, with Reynolds putting up the money. But, when Joe dropped around to the Clay household in Louisville with a contract for $75 a week for ten years, 'to be signed immediately', it was, Ali later recorded, the first time his trainer had ever visited his family. And the last. As Cash reportedly told Martin, bidding him adieu, 'Nobody buys my son for seventy-five dollars a week for ten years! The slave trade is over!'

But was it really? Is it really? Slavery comes in shades of subservience. So Clay went to work for

Reynolds, an hour's bus ride from town, after doing his roadwork in the early morning around Chickasaw State Park and spending two hours in the gym (with Martin just guiding the punches now). Cassius still called older people, 'Sir', black or white. He imagined he might get a job on the Reynolds estate using the mechanical drawing skills of which he'd learnt a little with his father. That didn't happen. For several weeks, he did not even meet Reynolds. He got a job all right, though: shifting garbage, scrubbing floors, mopping up toilets, sweeping porches, trimming hedges, cleaning windows.

Now, even if Ali's version of his awakening to the white adult world of Louisville in the early 1960s has been dressed up to suit a subsequent agenda, the story rings true of the times. It is not only perfectly believable but daft to refute. This was the Louisville Cassius Clay returned to as a young black Olympic champion, imagining his defeat of Mr Because and all the others was going to open many doors for him.

Joe Martin was not the only one desperate to sign Clay. Offers came in from old champions Archie Moore and Rocky Marciano, as well as Cus D'Amato, who'd taken Floyd Patterson to the title (and would later tutor a young Mike Tyson), and even Pete Rademacher, the former Olympic champion whose first professional fight was to challenge Patterson for his world title. Pete was knocked out in six rounds. Perhaps not best to go with Pete.

Clay's proper, signed and sealed introduction to the benign aristocracy of his old and very white home town was with the group who would control the early part of his career: ten (later eleven) rich, conservative patriarchs, leading lights of Kentucky old money who would be known in the young fighter's narrative as the Louisville Sponsoring Group. The deal was for six years, with $10,000 upfront and a fifty–fifty split of all earnings. As Clay recalled, the house they grew up in cost his father $4,500 and took him a lifetime to pay for. He signed – and with part of his first fee, he bought his mother a pink Cadillac.

This has resonance in black culture, especially post-war. The very fine movie *Cadillac Records* faithfully records the history of Chess Records, cofounded by a Polish Jewish immigrant, Leonard Chess, and which gave a platform to such wonderful black artists as Chuck Berry, Etta James, Howlin' Wolf, Muddy Waters, Little Walter and Willie Dixon. To ensure their loyalty, Chess gave each of them a Cadillac, the very symbol of American 1950s affluence and style. It was like a prize for being cool, greater than cash – even if it was worth less than the contract might have dictated. But Clay needed no favours from his loving mother. There was nothing in it for him. He would discover over the years, however, that such gifts, in cash or kind, often disguised a ruse.

Clay was now part of the Establishment. But he wasn't cleaning any more toilets. And he remembers how his people responded. 'The Sunday after I signed, the Reverend Isaiah Brayden, of the Ship of Zion Baptist Church, preached a sermon about it, and said, "May Cassius Clay be eternally grateful for what those kind Christian millionaires are doing for his black soul." Every newspaper account had described the event in the holiest light, with ten white angels tending charity in the jungle. Not as the good, hard, common-sense business deal it was.'

That is such a revealing insight. At the time, Clay and his father were satisfied they had made the right business choice, and regarded it as just that; but everyone else had another take on it. The alternative view was that these kind, white missionaries were saving the young black boxer from himself. They would guide him to the Promised Land. They would not let him fall among thieves. They would save not just his black ass but his soul. Hallelujah!

Whether they regarded their investment so is doubtful. For all that they represented their version of white goodness and southern values, they were businessmen, albeit well-meaning and proud of their city's finest fighter. They hoped to make a return and also to accompany their new thoroughbred through the winner's circle, bathing in the light of his glory. Nobody in the history of patrons of the noble art had ever sponsored a fist fighter for mere good intentions.

The Duke of Cumberland, the son of George II, probably set the benchmark in disdainful cruelty that a thousand managers since would struggle to match when he abandoned his champion Jack Broughton after a bare-knuckle fight in 1750. Broughton, a former champion of England, had come out of retirement to fight a Norwich butcher called Jack Slack, whose youth and vigour were too much for him. When young Jack planted several heavy blows on old Jack's battered face, he left him helpless and temporarily blind, beaten, humiliated and calling out to his master, 'I cannot see my Lord, I cannot see.' Cumberland, known as the Butcher of Culloden for his brutal suppression of the Jacobite rising there four years earlier, lost £10,000 in wagering on Broughton in that fight, and turned away from his man, disgusted. They never spoke again.

They were all, then, pawns in the greed business. Joe Martin knew that and so did the Louisville Sponsoring Group; as did Clay, of course. He wanted his hit record. But he was still an innocent, full of life and expectation, hoping that his career in boxing would lead him on to a Promised Land, somewhere better than the small house he had grown up in on Grand Avenue with his loving but struggling family.

How tough was that struggle? One prominent and recent revisionist, Jack Cashill, who grew up white and poor in Jersey, casts doubt on the view that the young fighter came from grinding poverty, or was even working class, and disputes the long-held belief that Clay was the grandson of a slave.

This latter quibble is not worth dissecting in detail here, as its authenticity or otherwise is not immediately relevant to our view of the person Clay/Ali became. If it were true, so be it; if it were not strictly true (and the arguments are convoluted and complicated), it hardly disqualifies him from claiming allegiance to a tradition of racial struggle. That Cashill brings it up at all says more about his agenda – to deconstruct the Ali myth – than it does about Clay's clinging to that story as true. It is a bit like being told that the stories your family handed down to you were lies, or at least would not survive intense scrutiny, and therefore your legitimacy as part of that story was diminished.

Of more relevance are Clay's immediate circumstances in a black community in a white, southern city in the 1950s and 1960s – because that is what shaped him. In *Sucker Punch*, mentioned earlier, Cashill disagrees with academic and social historian Joyce Carol Oates that Clay was (in Cashill's words), 'a victim of America'.

He writes: 'For all the maddening indignities of the pre-civil rights South, Ali was born into a life more secure and comfortable than that of almost any child anywhere in the world.' If you stand back from that assertion for a second, its nonsense hits you between the eyes like a Sonny Liston jab. Cashill continues: 'Neither Oates nor others of her literary caste would give Kentucky, or even America, credit for that. Instead, they encouraged Ali to reject his heritage and to repudiate its gifts – his faith, his country, even his name.'

Cashill calls up as a witness Clay's father, Cassius Snr, to prove his case as a decent, hardworking parent of two sons, Cassius and Rudolph: 'I dressed them up as good as I could afford, kept them in pretty good clothes. And they didn't come out of no ghetto. I raised them on the best street I could afford: 3302 Grand Avenue in the West End of Louisville.'

I went to that house. And I can tell you there's not a lot grand about Grand Avenue. The Clays had long left when I visited a decade or so ago. It was a small, neat bungalow in an unprepossessing street. The roof on the veranda had collapsed (as it had done when the Clays lived there), and weeds sprouted here and there. True, this was no ghetto, but it was the sort of tough neighbourhood Cashill should have been familiar with. The West End of Louisville is more like the East End of London than any Grand Avenue I've ever seen.

However, Cashill was not done with Clay the working-class hero. To support his case, he also called up Ferdie Pacheco, whom he describes as 'the esteemed ring doctor', crediting him with having written 'arguably the most intimate and insightful of all books on Ali', a claim some other chroniclers of the Ali tale might dispute, notably Thomas Hauser, who compiled the definitive collection of first-hand interviews with hundreds of people who knew Ali, some of them every bit as familiar with Ali as Pacheco was.

Anyway, Pacheco's take on Clay's young life fits with Cashill's. He was, reckoned Pacheco, 'distinctly middle class', adding: 'They lived in a nice house ... the children, Cassius and Rudy, dressed well and went to a good school. The problems of the ghetto were alien to them.'

What is odd about this debate is that it exists at all. In striving to rewrite the accepted version of Clay's upbringing and to paint the son of a hard-drinking, often out-of-work sign writer (or 'skilled muralist', as Cashill would have it), and pointing to the fact that he had an uncle who was a mathematician and a maths teacher for an aunt, Cashill patronises his subject. He goes to considerable lengths to prove that links to a slave heritage are tenuous. He describes the representation of Clay/Ali in the sympathetic terms employed by Oates and other supposed liberals as part of the 'grievance narrative' in the American media. This, he says, smacks hard of guilt, of over-compensating for past sins, of being naïve in accepting tales of woe from black individuals who, Cashill asserts, are actually members of the finest democracy in the world, lucky post-war recipients of the trickle-down wealth in the richest country on the planet.

In 1960, white Louisville took to Clay wholeheartedly, the way Cashill would have liked. At a rally organised by the mayor, Clay was made to recount in front of a wholly white audience what he had said to a Russian at the Olympics who had asked what life was like in America for blacks. He cringed as the mayor paraphrased his response for him: 'Look here, Commie. America is the best country in the world, including yours. I'd rather live here in Louisville than in Africa, 'cause at least I ain't fightin' off no snakes and alligators and livin' in mud huts.' In the jungle of clichés, there was no shortage of quick-hit vipers in the American storytelling tradition.

He has always maintained he was talking out of naivety, from 'Tarzan movies' knowledge of Africa, and he later observed, 'It took me a while to learn that while the slave masters cheer for slavery, they get a freakish thrill making the slave cheer for slavery too.' That must have been a crushing experience for a young black athlete to go through in his home town, accepting the applause of an audience who condescended to accept him as what he described as, 'a black white hope', their brown-skinned hero, as long as he played the game, read from their script, agreed with their world view. He knew little better then; but all that would change – and it started with one incident that has become a central plank of his legend.

The next lesson Clay was to learn in cynicism had nothing to do with money or applause. It hit him hard, suddenly and is shrouded in myth. As he remembers it, and as it has been passed down as if on tablets of stone, it started in a roadside café shortly after the mayoral reception that had left him feeling dirty inside, ashamed of letting himself be portrayed as their honorary white boy.

When Cassius and his friend Ronnie King rolled their bikes up alongside a row of Harley-Davidson hogs, they suspected it might have been a foolish move. When they walked into the café and saw the Confederate flags pasted across the leather jackets of the bikers inside, they definitely knew this was the wrong place to be, a suspicion that was confirmed when the young white girl serving whispered apologetically, 'We can't serve you.' Up to this point, the story rings unerringly true. There were still many segregated restaurants, bars and cafés across the Deep South, and especially in Louisville. The divide was unspoken and adhered to, in the main – although, if you go with the Cashill and Pacheco versions of 1960s America, Clay should have been grateful growing up in a land of milk, honey, money and opportunity. But Clay was not in the mood to be patronised anymore. He'd had it with the mayor that afternoon and he was going to make a stand. The reason the story has a ring of authenticity about it is that, in his authorised version of it, Clay identifies people in the café that he knew – guys like Kentucky Slim and Frog, whom he'd seen at his fights, and who'd nodded towards him when he and Ronnie walked in. But, according to Clay, they were not on nodding terms now. They had opened up a line of hostility and there was going to be a fight. What happens from this point onwards in the story has become a matter of rolling conjecture ever since.

Clay was wearing his gold medal, he maintains. He had just been to the mayor's office, so it made sense. It also fitted the wider version of his attachment to the bauble, that he slept with it under his pillow, so proud was he still of his achievement on behalf of his country. So, the chain of events suggest he might well have had the medal with him that day. He told the waitress he was Cassius Clay, the Olympic light-heavyweight boxing champion, and he showed her the gold medal to prove it. She was, he said, impressed. Kentucky Slim, Frog and his friends were not. Nor was the white, male owner. 'We don't serve niggers!' he shouted at them.

As Clay recalls it: 'Never in a hundred fights did I feel blood rushing to my head as I did then.'

Ronnie, wrote Clay, had a pearl-handled switchblade in his pocket, 'a long wicked weapon he'd taken off a dying pimp, "Jailhouse Sydney Green – meanest pimp I ever seen" ...' This version was now ambling towards the surreal. We were on a movie set of someone's imagining, either Ali or his ghost writer Durham. But the real drama was still to come.

As he has it in his book, Clay still had in his pocket the list of names of all his rich white sponsors, a piece of paper to prove his legitimacy as a coming champion of the world, because he had their approval and backing. It smacked of childish trust, but that is what he said. So he took out the list and moved towards the phone box in the café to call one of his benefactors, so they could prove to this pig-ignorant owner and the Nazi-regalia-clad bikers that he really was the Olympic champion, Louisville's representative in the land of the Roman gladiators.

He looked at the piece of paper and read down the list: James Ross Todd, the youngest of them at twenty-two; William Faversham Jnr, the main man and the expatriate son of an English actor; William Lee Lyons Brown, the man whose family business was Brown-Forman, owner of Jack Daniel's bourbon; George W. Norton IV, a horse breeder descended from Martha Washington; Patrick Calhoun Jnr, a boating millionaire; Archibald McGhee Foster, a northerner; William Sol Cutchins, a tobacco man and direct descendant of a Confederate general; Vertner DeGarmo Smith and Robert Worth Bingham, newspaper owners; J.D.S. Coleman, another oil tycoon; and, finally, Elbert Gary Sutcliffe, whose family ran US Steel.

He rang the last number. But he couldn't tell him why, so he hung up. Clay and King looked back to face the room of hostile white faces. 'My Olympic honeymoon was over,' he would write later. As they went to leave, an old black woman came out of the kitchen and pressed into his hand a copy of a poem he'd written for one of the black newspapers after winning his gold medal. In part it read, 'I said I appreciate kind hospitality; But the USA is my country still; 'Cause they waiting to welcome me in Louisville'.

For many this tale is already too perfect, like a scene from a movie. If so there could be a good reason for that. Richard Durham, the ghost writer of Ali's book *The Greatest* ..., was also a screenwriter.

Durham is a fascinating man, little understood – or much known, for that matter. To understand Ali's autobiography, it is important to understand the man who put the words together on a printed page (because that was something the loquacious Ali was not able to do). Much hangs on his credibility and it is unfair to proceed further to judgment on Durham and Ali without looking briefly at the speaker's voice.

Durham was born in 1917 into a small rural community, Raymond in Hinds County, Mississippi, the son of a farmer who took the family to Chicago in the early 1920s. He did well enough to get into Northwestern University, where he was drawn to a programme for prospective writers. It was there he learnt how to write for radio, which was fast becoming the media of the masses.

Echoing Ali's serendipitous introduction to boxing, Durham only became a career writer after an accident while working cleaning blinds in an industrial plant. He stepped into a skin-burning chemical in shoes that were not waterproof and, during his rehabilitation, began writing poetry on a typewriter that his sister gave him. He won a poetry prize and was offered scriptwriting work on a Chicago radio station. From that moment, he became deeply involved in politics and civil rights.

Durham first came to prominent notice in the African-American community in 1948 when he wrote *Destination Freedom*, a radio play that ran on Chicago station WMAQ. It was a vocal account of prominent African-Americans such as Satchel Paige, the poets Ralph J. Bunche and Langston Hughes and, inevitably, Joe Louis.

For two years, he wrote scripts for the programme, unpaid, and lived with the threats and intimidation of all the familiar white supremacist groups, such as the Knights of Columbus and the Ku Klux Klan. Only recently have tapes of the radio show come to light. What is clear from listening to some of them is that Durham wrote with passion and conviction. He also wrote a black soap opera, *Here Comes Tomorrow*.

In the 1950s, he wrote pamphlets for the United Packinghouse Workers of America, highlighting their work in fighting discrimination against minorities, and working in their cause for equal pay for women. He was without doubt a progressive and, as such, will have come under serious scrutiny in the age of McCarthyism. He resigned from the union in 1957 when he hit a roadblock over racial equality, however.

From there, through the precariousness of more freelance journalism, he ended up in the arms of the Nation of Islam and in the turbulent 1960s became editor of *Muhammad Speaks*, the mouthpiece of the movement's dictatorial leader, Elijah Muhammad, the man who would have such a profound impact on the boxing career and life of Muhammad Ali.

As his writing career blossomed and political convictions deepened, Durham also found television. He was the creator of the ground-breaking *Bird of the Iron Feather*, an all-black production of writers and actors, and hugely popular during the few months it lasted in 1970. The title was borrowed from a speech by the eloquent abolitionist Frederick Douglass in 1847 in which he likened an enslaved black man to, 'a bird for the hunter's gun, but a bird of iron feathers, unable to fly to freedom'.

It was in his capacity as editor of *Muhammad Speaks*, however, that Durham was asked to write Ali's book in the mid-1970s, as his boxing career was beginning to disintegrate. Durham was always an adversarial writer, identifiably of the left, a polemicist through stories. 'The real-life story of a single Negro in Alabama walking into a voting booth across a Ku Klux Klan line has more drama and world implications than all the stereotypes Hollywood or radio can turn out in a thousand years,' he once said. It is this gift that shines through *The Greatest* .... It reads with compelling pace and drama like a racy novel – yet inasmuch it is Ali's real story relayed through Durham, there are plenty of sceptics who doubt Durham's reliability as a ghost writer as opposed to a playwright. They wonder about the detail, given there is so much of it. Did he embellish incidents for effect? Or did Ali prove to be the most co-operative subject, sharing with Durham the minutiae of his life, complete with colourful dialogue?

What his critics have thrown at Durham down the years is his involvement with the Nation of Islam, painting him as little more than a cheerleader for a group that drifted from religion to the most aggressive political stance, uncompromising in its support of separatism to the point where they briefly joined common purpose with the hated Klan. His ghosting of Ali's approved autobiography will always fall under that cloud, fairly or not. But that is to ignore his other talent: writing and his keen eye for injustice. Whether his forensic skills matched his imagination we will probably never know, as he was relying wholly on the integrity of the evidence that was presented to him, given he was not there to see it for himself.

Durham's version of the now famous confrontation in the biker's café has been called into question in that context, but it cannot be dismissed out of hand. Whatever the authenticity of the episode, it surely has the ring of truth about it. What it also has, unfortunately, is a patina of radio-show theatricals – especially at its denouement, not helped by Davis Miller's claim that Ali told him years later it was nonsense.

To return to the Durham version: with Ronnie now swearing loudly at their antagonists, pearl-handled knife at the ready, they made their Wild West retreat from the saloon. As they got to the car park, they heard footsteps: it was the white waitress and another white customer. They said they wanted an autograph. Maybe they did, but then came the bad guys, shouting abuse at 'Olympic nigger' and his friend.

Kentucky Slim, the sort of good bad guy, told Clay that Frog wanted a souvenir for his girl, 'that there ribbon and the medal', then he allowed, they could 'go on 'bout your business'. There was an echo of a thousand such Hollywood confrontations here, most starkly the showdown between Marlon Brando and the Mob on the docks of New York in *On the Waterfront*, the ultimate confrontation of right and wrong, an image Durham would have had at the front of his consciousness, no doubt.

There follows in *The Greatest* ... an extended, word-for-word exchange leading on to the inevitable final scene. It was raining, of course, as the dark mood demanded. Clay was a few days out from making his professional debut at Louisville's Freedom Hall, of all places. The hogs circled our cornered heroes, taunting them racially. Clay decided he would outsmart Slim and Frog and his evil pack by heading for Jefferson County Bridge, in the opposite direction from the safety of the black part of Louisville, and over the border, with a view to doubling back across one of the other bridges on the river.

The chase began. Clay was glad to have Ronnie with him. He was, Clay reckoned, 'a natural demon by street rules'. They reached the bridge, reckoning they had given the chasers the slip. They had not. Frog pulled alongside them, 'whirling his chain'. Ronnie got out of his saddle, flinging his bike under Frog's. They crashed, Frog, bike and his girl. Slim, at full gallop on his Harley, thrashed at Clay with his chain. Clay grabbed it, dragging him towards a collision. Their heads clashed, Clay struck him hard in the face, and down he went.

The rest of the posse, oddly, had arrived late and were now encouraged to hang back, as their leaders were getting smashed by Clay and Ronnie, Frog's girlfriend screaming all the while. The bad guys limped away, into the rain. The winners soothed their wounds and washed the blood away, down by the river. Clay hung his medal on a pier 'thick with Frog's blood'. Ronnie washed the blood from it and Clay mused that this was the first time it had been out of his grasp since he won it. 'It had lost its magic,' he remembered. He walked to the centre of the bridge, cut the ribbon from the medal and, with Ronnie running towards him, begging him not to do what the script now demanded he do, Clay, 'threw it into the black water of the Ohio'. He recalls that he 'watched it drag the red, white and blue ribbon down to the bottom behind it'. It was a scene unbearably heavy in symbolism, the final sacrifice of honour, the cutting of the bond between the past and what might lie ahead. 'We don't need it,' he told Ronnie. 'We don't need it.'

And so was set in the mud of an old river, preserved forever, an unverifiable story, one moving enough to start a revolution. There would be no reconciliation with white America now. This would be the turning point, a reference point for the future. If that medal did sink to the depths of the river, it was weighed down with poignancy.

As for what Durham thinks, we cannot know. He died in 1984 while researching the life of Hannibal, the Carthaginian warrior who marched an army of elephants over the Pyrenees. On Ali's own website, meanwhile, there is no mention at all now of the medal being flung into the murky waters of unverifiable history. The entry for September 1960 ends simply: 'Despite his accomplishments for the US, he is denied service in a segregated restaurant in Kentucky'.

The excellent American boxing writer, Jerry Izenberg, when asked if he thought the story of the abandoned medal were true, arched a greying eyebrow and replied, 'If they trawled the Ohio River for a thousand years, they'd more likely find a mermaid than an Olympic gold medal.' When I asked the promoter Don King the same question many years later, he chuckled in his conspiratorial way and said, 'That's what they say, young man. That's what they say. Heh, heh!'

So, who knows? Only one man – and he doesn't say much anymore …

Chapter Four
'The Posture of Your Blows are Yet Unknown'

'What are you doing in there?' my mother would ask, as I rolled my shoulders and danced from one foot to the other in her bedroom, in front of the only mirror in the house, throwing punches from all angles at what I imagined must have been barely visible speed.

'I'm beating up Sonny Liston – what do you think I'm doing?' I would reply. Sonny stood no chance. I rifled him with jabs and crosses, then moved out of range (banging into the bedside table now and again), hands held low and feet skimming over the linoleum, before I delivered the final chilling right cross, bang on the side of his jaw and Sonny twirled from the ankle and slid crazily to the floor, unable and unwilling to get up. I stood above his writhing form, eyes on fire, mouth open wide, ready to say something ridiculous and then ... as I went airborne and attempted to scissor my feet, my lie kicked in. The feet got stuck. I fell to earth. Right next to Sonny. For a dreadful second, I thought he might then wink at me, get up, laugh like the baddie I knew him to be and put me in hospital.

Once I had been the champ, Floyd Patterson, but I tired of him. Anyway, within a few years, Sonny would beat up Floyd, and he never said much. Mum liked him, I think, because he became a Catholic. She even bought me a *Classics Illustrated* comic about him, illustrating the wonderful tale of the local priest who saw good in the young tearaway and turned him into one of those quiet, holy kids who could have gone on to be Pope, or at least a bishop. I never knew Joe Louis, I have to admit. By the time I was becoming heavyweight champion of the world, Joe had lost most of his hair and I couldn't understand everything he said. Archie Moore? Rocky Marciano? Jersey Joe Walcott? They were other old guys. They were dad's fighters, and my uncles'. This new guy, Cassius Clay, he belonged to me. He never shut up. I found it harder to be Clay than I had done being Floyd. I couldn't do his shuffle, I made a mess of his accent and I didn't get his poems. But nobody else knew that. What I knew was that Cassius wanted to fight Sonny – and so did I.

Growing up being Cassius in a small town in Australia was a thrill. He never seemed to grow old. So, as you got older yourself, you got closer to him. In front of the mirror in your parents' bedroom, you beat everybody. I sometimes wondered how many kids around the world were throwing the same punches – except not as fast, of course. Long before my sport went totally nuts and gave titles away like free T-shirts, each continent boasting its own set of suits to govern the business, each of them denying the existence of the other, all of them pathetically out of touch with the worldwide mood of revulsion at their ego-inspired blindness to the degradation of professional boxing, I had a title. I was the undisputed champion of the mirror in my mother's bedroom.

And then more reality kicked in. At the Maitland Police and Citizens Boys' Club – otherwise known as Madison Square Garden in my head – there was a single ring which, from memory, seemed enormous but probably wasn't. The ropes were always slack and the canvas a smeared grey colour that never got clean. There were speckles of red here and there, too. The turnbuckle was a comforting padded thing to lean against before you bounced along the ropes, testing their scary elasticity with your unprotected back ahead of defending the world heavyweight title in front of, er, a couple of mates. The gloves were enormous, at least half a stone, it seemed, coloured deep, deep claret or sometimes brown, and cracked roughly where your little knuckles would be under a mountain of compressed horse hair. They came half way up your arm too, which I never understood at the time, because they never looked like that on Cassius. And his shorts, shiny and white with a black stripe down each side, seemed to fit perfectly. My stiff cotton blue rugby shorts, with pockets inside where we'd put a bit of thin sponge for some unknown reason, just about reached my knees, leaving about six inches from the hem to the top of my sneakers. We had no proper boxing boots or headgear. Ha! As if we'd even need such protection. What was the point of climbing inside one of those foolish hats if the punches that landed on your head could barely disturb the neat parting in your Brylcreemed hair?

And then came the right cross. I can't remember the owner's name, but he had snowy white hair and, by some miracle, he was smaller than me. Neither of us weighed even five stone. Together, we might have made a decent doorstop. But the little guy swung from somewhere I had never noticed before – behind his back – and bowled his giant right glove through my own giant gloves, confounding my normally cat-like reflexes and landing it on to my conk. The explosion of very old leather on a very young and, dare I say, pretty, nose produced a warm flow of pumping red blood. The crimson waterfall spilled down past my mouth on to my singlet, which housed a chest of several bones and maybe a couple of muscles to hold them in place. So baggy was the singlet, the blood managed to drip inside of it on to the hairless expanse of undeveloped white skin that I called a chest. I recall swaying slightly and then not seeing my assailant. He had somehow moved to my side. As I began to adjust my feet in readiness for a counter assault of horrific proportions, one knee betrayed me and I lurched at a weird angle, my head now somehow level with the top of his shorts, also cotton and blue and baggy – probably from the same shop. As I heard more swishing above, I rose to my full height of about 5ft 3in, and walked into another of these unguided missiles. The collision had the effect of spinning me in a completely new direction, looking straight at Constable Terry Finch, the officer who had been assigned to instruct us in the art of fisticuffs – except there seemed to be two of him … or at least two heads on the same set of shoulders, both grinning as if he were watching a Laurel and Hardy movie. As the bell went, signalling the end of the combat, he leaned over the ropes, hauling me in as if I had just survived the sinking of the *Titanic*, and apparently said something in English, but it sounded as if he were mumbling into his handkerchief, which doubled as a face wipe. What he was saying, I later discovered, was, 'I think that's enough for today, son.' As he cleaned up my nose, which now seemed to be volunteering blood like some local branch of the Red Cross, I felt like whacking him. Or someone. Anyone. Ah, what about Snowy? Where the bloody hell had he gone?

That, right there, was my world heavyweight title fight. There would be other minor bouts, casually arranged spars with schoolmates from Maitland Marist Brothers in the same little ring, watched by nobody but us. Nothing, though, would match the drama of that afternoon, a bout that somehow escaped chronicling in *The Ring*, which curiously used to arrive several months late at our local newsagent's yet had the right month's date on it, making it about as up to date as the hymns we sang in mass. I was an altar boy, as well, naturally. My mother said Floyd would have been an altar boy, had he not been out stealing fruit in some bad neighbourhood. Oh, how I wanted to steal some fruit.

The year was 1960 and, in the Freedom Hall in Louisville, on 29 October – just a month or so after Clay had supposedly thrown his Olympic gold medal away in a fit of repressed anger – into the ring stepped a boxer who might otherwise never have been even a trivia question but for the fact he was Cassius Clay's first professional opponent.

Clay would have happily fought Sonny Liston for the title that night, but he had to start in a more humble manner. Tunney Hunsaker had a handle that deserved to be remembered, his parents having named him after the former world heavyweight champion, Gene Tunney. The schoolteacher and police officer – who was no more Gene Tunney than I was Cassius Clay – went six rounds with the eighteen-year-old Olympic champion that day in Louisville's State Fairground, paying for the privilege with lots of blood in the main bout of a three-fight bill, but getting to the final bell in front of a paying audience of more than 6,000, whose hard-earned admission money went to the fighters, naturally, and to the Kosair Crippled Children's Hospital. It was not the last time Clay would fight for a hospital. It was, though, the last time we would wonder about Mr Hunsaker, who had travelled from Fayetteville, West Virginia, and finished with both his eyes closing on him and a miserable scorecard to take home, Clay winning every round. 'He was as fast as lightning,' said Hunsaker, who was not. A nice man, Hunsaker would lose five of his remaining seven fights, retiring in 1962 after Joe 'Shotgun' Sheldon knocked him out in ten rounds. He spent nine days in a coma, coming round after two brain operations, and remained friends with the kid from Louisville until he died at seventy-five in 2005, after being treated for Alzheimer's at the end of his life. Ali, unannounced, came to his police retirement party in Fayetteville. Tunney Hunsaker has a bridge named after him in West Virginia – and quite right, too.

Every fighter Clay/Ali fought had a story, some of them hilarious, some ordinary, some ineffably sad. None could match that of the man himself, but there were many opponents such as Hunsaker, who battled in anonymity, mainly, and were allowed into the sunlight of Ali's world for the briefest glimpse of glory.

I have vague memories of finding out about the Hunsaker fight – a day or so later, I think, in a very short story in the local newspaper – where I would start my own writing career. I do not remember hearing about it on TV or the radio. That media storm was to come. In 1960, when I was ten, and still could not do what was going to become known as the Ali Shuffle, life in small-town Australia was quiet beyond imagining, apart from the odd scrap on the way home from school with kids who did not know I was Cassius Clay.

Who did not love the name Cassius? The films of the day, from the 1950s into the early 1960s, were quite often sandal-and-toga epics, mostly set in Rome, with Hollywood stars with (weirdly) blue hair pretending to be senators or Caesar himself, or gladiators clattering around the Colosseum in chariots with spiked wheels. The women were always blessed with the pointiest breasts, pressing with cantilevered encouragement through thin white tops, clasped at the waist with golden rope and encouraging the sort of fantasies that could send a young Catholic boy into a hell of guilt. My favourite movie of the time, and for many years after, was *The Vikings*, starring Tony Curtis, who uttered the immortal line in an impeccable Bronx accent, 'Yonder lies da cassle o' my fadda.' But Cassius: what a name. We knew it in Shakespeare and in the movies and it was something your mouth could swallow and devour. I remember the first time I heard it I wanted it for myself. Except this guy Clay had it. I was stuck with Kevin.

Unless you had the faraway thrill of watching Clay grow up on your black-and-white television screen, it is difficult to convey what a powerful experience it all was. He was immense in every way. Indeed, he was as big as you wanted to make him because he seemed to be exactly the same as all the other stars who filled the little screen. He wasn't just a boxer, he walked in different shoes. He shouted – God, how he shouted. I couldn't be sure if I'd ever heard of Louisville before someone had attached the name of that city to the word 'Lip', giving Cassius another identity. Nearly every time he made the news – which was so often back then it seemed like he was on some early version of a rolling news format – the second reference to him would be 'the Louisville Lip'. It sounded quite pretty, but I knew it was an insult. These guys who talked about him in faraway places did not like my friend Cassius. They seemed to know more about what he was really like than he did himself, because they kept telling us he was a loudmouth and he couldn't really box and, without question, he would be killed by Sonny Liston if they ever met.

To get there, he needed a trainer to go with his well-heeled management team and, after flirting with Archie Moore, he settled on one of boxing's characters, Angelo Dundee, a New York Italian who'd never boxed and whose brother, Chris, had links with the Mob. Frankie Carbo, Blinky Palermo and Jim Norris had the fight business in their grip in the 1950s through the International Boxing Club and an exclusive arrangement with Madison Square Garden, the sport's spiritual home, but Dundee was not part of that set-up at all; nor was his brother, Chris, but Chris 'knew people'. In boxing that was the sort of calling card that opened doors and Angelo and Chris fetched up in Miami to see what business they could do with an assortment of decent fighters – but none like the young man who barrelled into the gym one day demanding that Angelo take him on.

He'd met Dundee in Louisville when he came there with one of his star fighters, Willie Pastrano, and, as Dundee remembered it years later: 'We were in the hotel room when the phone rang. It was this kid: "Mr Dundee, my name is Cassius Clay." He gave me a long list of championships he was planning to win and wanted to come up to meet us. I put my hand over the mouthpiece and said to Willie, "There's a nut on the phone; he wants to meet you."' When they did meet, young Clay boxed Pastrano's ears off in the gym. It did not take Dundee long to agree to sign him. Theirs would be one of the rare enduring partnerships in a sport where treachery and double-dealing are common. Whatever the questionable judgment of Dundee in failing to protect Ali from himself in later years, the affection between them was genuine and unequivocal.

Those early years, before Clay became properly famous, are intriguing. At various points, the story might have been wrecked because boxing is a precarious trade. There are no guarantees and plenty of traps. So many fine boxers do not make it. Often it has little to do with their ability to box. Circumstances crowd in on them from all angles, with strangers and chancers constantly looking to muscle in on the show. Managers sell little slices of their property to people the fighter might never even meet, only to discover years later he is part-owned by some shady association of hoodlums. Professional boxing is full of front men and messengers, people willing to do the dirty work of others for a fee. It is far from glamorous. Often the dividend for these second and third parties is miniscule, but they are happy to be involved because it is what they do. They are bit players in a bigger story. And no story would become bigger than that of the young man from Louisville.

In 1961, the year he hooked up with Dundee, Clay was growing in confidence but still largely unformed. The raw material was there, ready to be shaped – and a chance meeting with a wrestler in June of that year was to play a significant part in turning the innocent young fighter into one of increasing bombast. Cassius never doubted he was going to be a champion and would tell anyone within earshot that it was only a matter of time before the rest of the world would come to agree with him. But they were not listening in those early days. The louder he shouted, the less they were inclined to pay him any attention at all.

But he would not be deterred. On a trip to Las Vegas, he met a character almost as outrageous as himself, the professional wrestler, 'Gorgeous George' Wagner, who, in the tradition of his very theatrical sport, was a loud and extravagant presence. When Clay saw George shouting about an opponent, 'I'll kill him! I'll tear his arms off!', he knew it was the language of baloney that attended pro wrestling, but he was captivated by George's style. And Clay made a business decision: 'I decided that if I talked like that, there was no telling how much money people would pay to see me fight.' One way or another, Gorgeous George has a lot to answer for.

From that point on, Clay became a showman. He did not just turn up for a fight and beat his opponent in style. He began telling everyone how great he was. Not just great: The Greatest. He was at least as great as Gorgeous George, he reckoned, and he wanted everyone to know it. Slowly, they began to listen. They could hardly avoid doing so: Clay was a ball of energy wherever he went, demanding attention from everyone he met, from people in the street to opponents in the ring. He broke tradition by engaging fighters in conversation not just before the bout but during it. As he told Michael Parkinson in a TV interview: 'You don't psyche 'em out, put fear in 'em. It makes 'em fight too hard. It makes 'em anxious. They gotta get ya. Like I told George [Foreman]: "Okay sucker, I'm backin' up on the ropes. I wanna take your best shots!" And I just stood there: "Come on, show me somethin'! Show me somethin', kid, you're not doin' nothin'. You're just a girl. Look at ya! You ain't got nothin'. Come on, sucker! Show me somethin'." [All the while Ali was mugging, holding his fists over his face, then opening them, peekaboo, like a kid playing a game.] If you think I'm not tellin' the truth, watch the film. I talked him to death! And I made him so angry, he just beat his self out. He was so tired, he was just flailin', fallin' on the ropes. I said to him, "Man, this is the wrong place to get tired!" I said, "You are in trouble! Didn't I tell you your hands can't hit what your eyes can't see? You know I'm The Greatest of all times." I tell him this when I get in clinches. That worries a man, to beat him and talk to him.'

Ali also drove referees to distraction and they often found themselves unable to control his outbursts. We all wondered, meanwhile: where did he get the energy? How could he fight and talk at the same time? His brother Rudy provided a clue from their childhood: 'All the time,' he said, 'he used to ask me to throw rocks at him. I thought he was crazy, but he'd dodge every one. No matter how many I threw, I could never hit him.' Throughout his life, Muhammad Ali invited people to throw rocks at him. Not many landed.

His boxing career followed a fairly conventional path for an Olympic gold medallist, the quality of the opponent slowly ramped up as he became used to the different demands and methods of the professional game.

After Hunsaker, they came and went in a blur until what might be regarded his first proper test, LaMar Clark, a 5ft 10in chicken farmer from Cedar City, Utah, who had the power of an ox and about as much ring sophistication. Clark's opponents were largely wrestlers or local have-a-go brawlers who made money on the 'tough man' circuit. In one night he knocked out five opponents in a row, all in the first round. They were not exactly classic boxing occasions.

Nevertheless, Clark turned up at the Freedom Hall with ambition and a record of forty-four consecutive knockouts, including one over Tony Burton, who would make a better living as an actor, including his role as a trainer, Duke, in the *Rocky* films. But LaMar's engagement with Clay was for real, and Cassius did to him what he did to Hunsaker:

he broke his nose, knocked him out and ended his career, at twenty-eight. He died in 2006, aged seventy-one.

Clay knew he would have to move more quickly through the ranks if he were to get his shot at Liston before the 'Big Bear', as he would come to call him, either was shot by his criminal friends or decided to retire. Nobody knew exactly how old Liston was, and not many were sure about the legality of his extra-curricular activities.

Meanwhile, I shadow-boxed on. At school, we would grind through the Bard's wisdom, and one phrase from Cassius, in *Julius Caesar*, stuck as I sparred pointlessly but happily in front of Mum's mirror: 'The posture of your blows are yet unknown'. You could say that again.

Chapter Five
But What Nation?

In 1964, like the loud kid on the street, Cassius got the fight he wanted, the one nearly everyone else in boxing did not want. He got the fight with Sonny Liston. A lot of people doubted his sanity and feared for his health – albeit they really did not care much what happened to him. He was to many an irritant, a curiosity. What they could not see, blinded by prejudice and indifference, was his brilliance. It would not take long for those scales to be lifted.

It had been four years since the Hunsaker fight. My own boxing 'career' was done. But the other guy called Cassius would soon be champion, of that I was sure. Yet I seemed to be only person in the world who thought so. What angered me was the barrage of hate that had descended upon Clay since Rome. Sure, he'd been loud, this Louisville Lip, but isn't that what they wanted, a bit of excitement, some flash?

This is what Jackie Gleason, the famous American comedian, general blowhard and paid-up barfly at Toots Shor's boxing hangout in New York, had to say before the fight between Clay and Liston in the Miami Beach Convention Center on 25 February 1964: 'I predict Sonny Liston will win in eighteen seconds of the first round, and my estimate includes the three seconds Blabber Mouth will bring into the ring with him.' It was funny. And it was sad.

Of course, Gleason and all the others didn't much like Sonny, either. So much hate, I remember thinking. Why can't these wise white guys, these American white fight writers and American white famous people just stop hating these very interesting black guys? Those were formative moments in my young life. I had stumbled across racism. It wasn't that funny.

I was, also, a little confused before this fight. Since Hunsaker, Clay had beaten another eighteen opponents, but there had been a couple of anxious moments. Sonny Banks had briefly floored him in 1962 – and 1963 had not gone entirely Clay's way. Doug Jones, a dangerous New Yorker, had hurt and inconvenienced him over ten rounds in the old Madison Square Garden in March, and Henry Cooper, an uncomplicated, craggy-faced Londoner with a killer left hook, had put him down and almost out of the whole picture at Wembley Stadium three months later, before his unreliable skin leaked an horrific amount of blood and he was retired. Those were not the performances of a god, those were human flaws. Why did I still think he could beat the fearsome Liston, who had lost just once in thirty-six fights, knocked out twenty-five opponents and recently had twice destroyed Floyd Patterson in a round?

I kept the faith. So, oddly, did my mother. Always a fan of the woebegone and disregarded (her favourite boxer was Freddie Mills, who had a face only a mother could love, and ended up dead, shot in the front seat of a car in a side street in London's red-light district in 1965), she had a soft spot for 'that Cassius boy', even when he was being outrageous. As did her brother, Dermot, who boxed to a good level in the Gardaí in Ireland. My father was not so sure. He thought Clay an upstart, too cheeky for his own good. But everyone had an opinion by this stage about Clay, who would soon become someone else. Then the divisions would go considerably deeper. Then we would see the man behind the fighter. Not everyone would like what was revealed. For now, he was the only fighter in the world worth worrying about – in my bedroom, anyway. I had a transistor radio by this time: what very heaven it was to be young with an earplug under a blanket on 25 February 1964.

The fight dripped with poignancy, not all of which I appreciated at the time. Liston had been champion only since September 1962 – that much I knew – when he knocked out poor Floyd Patterson in one round, repeating the beating ten months later, also in one round. This truly was an ogre. Everybody said so. Patterson didn't even want to fight him, although all of America did. Patterson, cleansed and walking in the shadow of Cus D'Amato, who had become venerated as some sort of white knight of boxing, knew he stood no chance against Sonny. Sonny knew it, we knew it, and so it came to pass. But Clay had been on Liston's case since the day he returned from Rome in 1960. He knew Patterson was only keeping the throne warm. He knew he would announce his arrival by beating Liston, not by easing past Patterson. Liston was the man: he was the one who was going to discover who was The Greatest. Then the world would have to listen. The problem was, the urge to get rid of Liston, the Mob's pet, did not manifest itself in any gathering support for the loud young Kentuckian. Clay was almost universally regarded as a talented clown. There was hardly a serious boxing writer who considered him capable of beating Liston – especially as he had been put on his backside in London by Henry Cooper, before getting up to shred the British fighter's frail eyebrows.

America, though, did not quite know what to do with Liston: to laugh at him or shiver in his presence. He confused people, and frightened them, so some writers tried to neuter his image, famously the clever people at *Esquire* magazine who put him on their Christmas cover in 1963 oozing menace while dressed as Santa Claus. But Liston was coming down nobody's chimney bearing presents that Yuletide. He brooded alone, retreating to the shadows with his underworld associates, where he felt most comfortable. He was inarticulate but he was brilliantly sharp. The man who'd learnt to box (but, contrary to legend, not to write) in prison, left us with a couple of very moving descriptions of his cruel calling.

After he beat Patterson, he was determined to be a champion his country and his sport could be proud of. His efforts were so wreathed in pathos as to make a grown man – or small boy – cry. I grew in time to admire Sonny Liston every bit as I loved Cassius Clay.

These are some of the things he said in public after he became world champion, a string of declarations that sounded as much like a plea for forgiveness as a statement of intent. 'Joe Louis was the greatest champion of all and my idol. He did everything I want to do. I intend to follow the example he set and would like to go down as a great champion too. When you reach your goal, you have to be proud and dignified. You represent something and you have a responsibility to live up to it. As champion, I have the opportunity to do things that otherwise might not be possible. I had nothing when I was a kid but a lot of brothers and sisters, a helpless mother, and a father who didn't care about any of us. I promise everyone that I will be a decent, respectable champion.'

Sad does not do his story justice. But every corner of life overflowed with melancholy. The guy never stood a chance – no matter how he tried to please white America, people who just plain hated his guts. The day after he had taken just two minutes and six seconds to put Floyd's lights out, he got on a plane to Philadelphia, certain that he was returning now as a lauded hero, respected at last, the heavyweight champion of the whole world. There would be a ticker-tape parade, he told one of his few reporter friends, Jack McKinley, there would be cheering and smiles and, finally, respect. When the plane door opened on to the tarmac, there was nobody. Nobody but reporters with pens poised for poison, still sniping at him, still wondering about his Mob connections, none of them there to shake his hand. McKinley swears he saw a tear on Liston's cheek. The reporter later told Bill Nack of *Sports Illustrated*: 'What happened in Philadelphia that day was a turning point in his life. He was still the bad guy. He was the personification of evil. And that's the way it was going to remain. He was devastated.'

Liston, hard in every other conceivable way, was wounded beyond repair. He left to live in Denver and uttered one of many beautiful statements about his own tortured existence and life in general: 'On the whole,' said the man who had to have his wife read the newspaper to him, 'I'd rather be a lamppost in Denver than the mayor of Philadelphia.' After Liston beat Patterson a second time, the ever-witty but not always wise *Los Angeles Times* sportswriter, Jim Murray, penned what he must have reckoned would be a sharp knockout blow of his own: 'The central fact is that the world of sport now realises it has gotten Charles Sonny Liston to keep. It is like finding a live bat on a string under your Christmas tree.'

That night, Ali, now on a full-scale propaganda assault, clambered into the ring and, for the first time, bellowed the anthem that would come to dominate boxing for a decade and more: 'I am The

Greatest! I am The Greatest! I am The Greatest! I am The Greatest!' He would not be silenced. And nobody wanted to listen to Liston, who, ten months after becoming the first challenger to knock out the world heavyweight champion in the first round, did it again.

Sonny Liston, the grown man with the kid's name, really was the champ nobody wanted. Nobody. Not the fans, his peers, the television executives. Would nobody rid them of this tempestuous devil?

But for all Ali's oratory and sense of occasion, however, it was Liston, the sharecropper's son (one of twenty-five children), the union-busting leg-cracker and ex-con, the man with the most feared left jab in the history of boxing, who would author the most moving description there has ever been of his grubby old art: 'Some day they're gonna write a blues for fighters. It'll just be for slow guitar, soft trumpet and a bell.'

José Torres, the erudite Puerto Rican light-heavyweight who also won a world title for D'Amato, and wrote in a beguilingly simple but wise way for a newspaper in his home country, once said: 'I have never met an athlete in baseball, basketball or football who is smarter, more intelligent than Sonny Liston.' But, like Joe Frazier, it was Liston's fate to be doomed to ridicule. And

Clay did little to alter that view of the man he would so humiliate in Miami that February.

What an occasion it was – and nobody saw it coming. It began at the weigh-in, the first time this otherwise routine segment of the boxing pageant was turned into a roaring farce. It took place – or, rather, unfurled – on the morning of the fight. Clay had already called Liston the 'Ugly Bear', a ritual of ridicule he would maintain for much of his career, and emblazoned on his denim jacket were the words 'Bear Huntin''. He also carried a walking stick. It was hilarious, madly so. And this was how his tirade went, uninterrupted by his opponent or pretty much anyone else: 'I'm the champ! Tell Sonny I'm here. Bring that big ugly bear on! Someone is going to die at ringside tonight! You're scared, chump!'

He was genuinely out of control. His heart rate doubled to 120 beats a minute. Sane people declared him mad. They thought he was going to have a heart attack. The commission said they would cancel the fight if his heart rate did not come down. The chief physician, Dr Alexander Robbins, said Clay was, 'emotionally unbalanced, scared to death, and liable to crack up before he enters the ring'. The commission fined him $2,500 – even more absurd: a governing body in boxing bothered about irresponsible behaviour.

And there really was method in his perceived madness. Clay calculated, correctly, that although Liston would already have regarded him lightly, now he had to deal with a man everyone said was not sane enough to be in a boxing ring. And Sonny, of all people, knew how mad that must be ...

These were the curious images, side by side, that the planet had of the world heavyweight title that day. The champion was someone who didn't have a friend outside his own house, the challenger was an ambulance ride away from being committed to an institution beforehand – or hospital with life-threatening injuries afterwards. While the combatants were a good deal smarter than that, the people who ran boxing were in despair: after the well-behaved Patterson, was this the best contest they could come up with to decide who would be the standard bearer of an enterprise that always struggled for respectability? Of course, they would have preferred a white champion, but one of those had not been available since Rocky Marciano retired and then died. They would have to settle for another black champion; but how they wanted him to be, well, not so 'uppity', the word they reserved for blacks on the rise, blacks who dared talk back, blacks who had the gumption and audacity to be themselves. Whatever their other strengths and weaknesses,

Clay and Liston very much were themselves – and white America did not like it one bit. When Clay would declare for the Nation of Islam and change his name, they would like it even less. They had already been softened up for this nightmare by an interview Clay's father, Cassius Snr, had given to the *Miami Herald* before the fight, in which he said: 'They [the Black Muslims, as they were popularly, or unpopularly, known] have been hammering at him ever since he joined when he was eighteen. He's so confused now that he doesn't even know where he's at. They ruined my two boys [Rudy had joined too]. Muslims tell my boys to hate white people; to hate women; to hate their mother.'

This was potent stuff. Nobody knew much about the 'Black Muslims'. Nobody knew much about regular Muslims. Dundee joked that he thought it was that stuff you put over the cheeseboard. These were troubling times all round for society and for the gentlemen in charge of the noble art. Clay cared not a jot. He would do what he was paid to do: fight. And he would be champion. He would kill that Ugly Bear. There would be, he said, 'a total eclipse of the Sonny'. Even in the middle of the serious business of upsetting an entire country, not to mention goading the most feared champion his sport had ever had, Clay found time for a daft joke. This would define his entire career, his life too. In his darkest moments, he never lost his gift for laughter, or for making others laugh. That is a rare quality. Some might say it pointed to a lack of clarity of thought, an inability to grasp cold, hard facts, to trivialise serious matters. But he always knew what he was laughing at – and it was invariably someone else.

The story of the fight is seared into modern popular consciousness: Clay dazzled Liston with his speed, frustrating him like nobody had ever done. For all that he was a late-blooming monster, he did have decent basic boxing skills, and a god-awful bone-breaking left hook, behind a jab that looked to opponents like an oak tree travelling at speed towards them down a dark alleyway with no exit. But the champion could land little of significance on his young tormentor. After three rounds he was doing the impossible: he was systematically beating on Sonny Liston. He was in front. He looked like he was going to win the fight, probably before the appointed end. This was surely not happening. Liston swished, Clay banged, exchange after exchange. The bruising under Sonny's eyes grew steadily. Would they envelope his sad face soon, ringsiders wondered? Would he get knocked out?

But then a twist: Clay returned to his corner at the end of round four and complained to Dundee that his eyes were burning so badly that he could not fight on, and to cut off the gloves. Dundee kidded him into going out for the fifth, unsure if he would get through the next three minutes but knowing it was better to try than quit, because then the whole world would laugh the laugh they'd been storing up for four years, to condemn his fighter as a fake, as some sort of worthless illusionist. Back to the fray went Clay and, boxing blind, survived. When his eyes cleared, he went back to work and it was Liston's turn to suffer again, outclassed, outsped, outpunched, out-thought. He was bamboozled and humiliated. Nobody had done this to him – not in public. His father, Tobe, a merciless man, would beat the hell out of him back in the hut, but here he was a grown man, a world champion, and the only real cache he had was the intimidation he brought into other people's lives. And now it was being taken away from him by this loud ballet dancer!

The fight that had been anticipated with all the enthusiasm of a street mugging ended up being *The Ring* magazine's Fight of the Year, and deservedly so. It was a brave, virtuoso performance by the young contender. All the talent he had came together on one night against a champion who had yet to show convincing signs of decline. And to watch Clay move was pure joy, nothing less. You did not have to like boxing to enjoy his gliding over the canvas, sometimes barely touching it, just letting his boots kiss it, as if floating. Like a butterfly, indeed. And he weighed 210 lbs. How was this possible? How could a man that big look so light, so perfect in flight? The image was strengthened as the man trying to put him in hospital chugged after him like an angered bull, snorting and pawing, but finding only air most of the time. Liston, it should not be forgotten, was a worthy and awesome champion. He deserved to hold the title because he was, for a couple of years, the best heavyweight in the world. But something gnawed at Liston, in and out of the ring. He carried so much baggage it is a wonder he was able to haul himself into the ring.

In the course of researching a book into boxing and the Mob in 2004, I visited an old fight face called Al Certo. Al, a former fighter, is now a trainer in Secaucus. Liston used to visit Al years ago. Al liked the guy, although he understood a lot of people didn't – especially the white fight writers – and Liston didn't much care for them, either.

'Upstairs here was my showroom,' Al told me that day, 'and Sonny Liston came in and he had all the reporters following him and they all knew Al Certo from Secaucus was a boxing guy and a former fighter, and all that bullshit. So they stopped in and he was looking at all these pictures and he said, "Where's all the black celebrities?" Well, I had a few up there so I'm showing him and then one of the reporters says to me, "We've been following him from Journal Square [in Union City, New Jersey] all the way to here, that's how far he'd walked, about three or four miles, and we can't get a word out of his mouth!" So I says, "Sonny, why don't you talk to the guys? They're trying to do a job, come on."'

'So I call the guys over and I said, "Ask him what you want." And a guy asks Sonny, "Well, what do you think you are going to do with Chuck Wepner [his upcoming opponent]?" And he was looking at the pictures and he said, "I'm gonna bust his fuckin' head." Just like that, and he said nuttin' more – and that's just what the hell he done.'

What Liston did to Chuck, he did to thirty-eight other guys in the fifty-four registered fights he had (one fewer than Ali) between 1953 and 1970. If he earned a lot of money, he spent a lot of money. He had a string of managers – Jack Nilon, Pep Barone, Eddie Polino, George Katz, Frank Mitchell, Dick Sadler. None of them was an angel, but nor was Sonny. He was just a fighter: nothing more, nothing less. Nobody was sure exactly where and when he was born; nor were they sure of the exact moment of his death, slumped at the bottom of his bed on

5 January 1970. He'd been dead for days. Some say the Mob killed him; some say he died of an overdose. Nobody knows and nobody, in all likelihood, ever will. That is the searing sadness of his story, because, ultimately, nobody really cared then and they don't much care now.

So, is it any wonder that we will never know why Sonny Liston chose not to rise from his stool at the start of round seven that day in Miami? The very good American writer, Dave Remnick, reported that someone in his corner heard Liston say, simply, 'That's it.' Well, maybe so. What preceded 'it'? What caused 'it'? Was it Mob interference? Was the fix in? Did his shoulder really give up on him? Once he'd capitulated, nobody gave a damn. Boxing had a new champion, and he would prove to be the most charismatic of them all, in stark counterpoint to the man he had just embarrassed.

What happened next was a ballet that might have been choreographed by Nureyev. Clay moved to centre ring, raised both arms at forty-five degrees, giving him the appearance of someone alighting from a crucifix, and danced his dance, his feet flashing in his famous shuffle, his eyes now wide open, a long, constant stream of babble morphing into sentences emanating from a mouth – that mouth, that infamous mouth – which was opened as wide as it ever can have been. The words tumbled over each other in a cacophony of self-adulation. 'I am the Greatest! I am the Greatest! I shook up the world! I shook up the world! I shook up the world!' At one point, it seemed he would never stop saying it, as if he would leave the ring, screaming, 'I shook up the world!', wake up the next morning and tell his team, 'I shook up the world!', go home to Louisville and tell his friends and family and strangers and enemies, anyone who'd listen, 'I shook up the world!'

And you know what? He pretty much did. And he was right: he shook up the world. Now, he reckoned the world had to listen. He was right there, too. Some people didn't want to listen. But they had no choice: he was the champ. And, more importantly, he was now Muhammad Ali. Whatever the reluctance of others to acquiesce to his demand that they call him by the name he wanted, he would from this point be Muhammad Ali. Cassius Clay was dead, long live Ali.

The birth of Ali was a very public one. In the maelstrom that followed his victory over Liston, he spoke at length, most uninterrupted, in a series of press conferences that proved to be pure theatre. Most of the fight writers present had never seen anything like this. The champions before Ali – as he now was – had been largely subservient. Interviews were short, clipped, managed, clichéd. The talking was left to the flamboyant promoters and managers, white guys – white guys with connections and dressed in expensive suits. Fighters wore shorts. Afterwards, they would sit in their dressing room, with their gowns around their shoulders and thank everybody who made it possible for them to put their lives on the line. In the aftermath of the first Liston fight, all that changed forever. This was the moment when the world really began to know Muhammad Ali.

As they followed him to the interview room, Ali regaled the writers. 'Waddya gonna say now? It won't last one round? He'll be out in two? How many heart attacks were there? Oh, I am pretty. I beat him bad and that's sooo good. The bear couldn't touch me, couldn't even get a lick of me.'

He even shut Jackie Gleason up. 'Ol' Cassius got his revenge on me without doing a thing,' he wrote in his *New York Post* column the next day. Pointedly, his Louisville backers had never believed he would beat Liston; they forgot to organise a victory party. When they did, at the last minute in the Roney Plaza, the celebrity writers Budd Schulberg, George Plimpton and Norman Mailer were prominent among the hastily gathered guests. Ali was not there, though. He chose to spend the evening with Malcolm X, still a noise in the Nation, and the American football star, Jim Brown – eating ice cream.

The next day, the media got another go at the champ. They can hardly have anticipated what he gave them. In long, well-structured monologues, Ali set down his case. He started slowly and built to a crescendo that would roll around the sports world, then further. It is worth looking at what he said, because he did not always stick by his creed, although there could be no doubting his sincerity at the time. He had been well tutored, by Malcolm X and others.

'All I want now is to be a nice, clean gentleman,' he began, sounding every bit like Joe Louis, who he would later castigate for his obsequiousness when managed by the boxing Establishment. It was a mere exploratory jab.

'I've proved my point,' he added. 'Now I'm going to set an example for all the nice boys and girls. I'm through talking.' Was he hell. After a pause, he continued: 'I only fight to make a living and, when I have enough money, I won't fight anymore. I don't like to fight. I don't like to get hurt. I don't like to hurt anybody. I feel sorry for Liston, he's all beat up.'

But then the elephant that had been sitting in the front row of the press conference all along arose and created an intellectual stampede. Asked to confirm that he had converted to Islam, Ali threw off the mantle of acquiescence. Now, he was a preacher. This was his first sermon. He would not let the opportunity slip by, because this was a higher calling than boxing, merely winning the world heavyweight title. This, he figured, was why he was here in the first place.

'I believe in Allah and peace. I don't try to move into white neighbourhoods. I don't want to marry a white woman. I was baptised when I was twelve but I didn't know what I was doing. I'm not a Christian anymore. I know where I'm going, and I know the truth, and I don't have to be what you want me to be. I'm free to be what I want.'

In that single powerful declaration, Ali set the tone for the rest of his life – 'I don't have to be what you want me to be. I'm free to be what I want.'

Cynics, of course, would later conclude that it wasn't so much Ali being who he wanted to be but what Elijah Muhammad and the Nation of Islam wanted him to be. And they observed that, so disdainful of his trade were the church's leaders, that their presence in his finest hour was limited to a few representatives. They did not expect him to win. They reckoned, along with Jackie Gleason and all the others, that Sonny Liston would beat him into obscurity and they would be left with very much an ex-contender. How wrong they were and how quickly they recognised their mistake. Soon, they were all over him. He was not just another preacher now; Ali was a brilliantly exploitable celebrity, one of the most famous in the whole world, and he could carry their message way beyond the hitherto very limited boundaries of their influence. They, like Ali, could conquer the world. He did not see the disparity in their relative power at the time. For Ali, the Nation was way bigger than he was, far more influential and important. Of course, he recognised what he had just achieved in a sporting context but his mindset was still subservience to Elijah Muhammad and it would remain that way for many years afterwards. His allegiance to a little-known, little-understood religion ensured he would continue to be alienated. That day after his triumph, he cared little for the consequences of his convictions.

He opened with something he plainly had picked up from someone else, a quasi-religious call to arms: 'A rooster crows only when it sees the light,' he told reporters who travelled out to the Hampton House motel, where he was staying. 'Put him in the dark and he'll never crow. I have seen the light and I'm crowing.'

This was regular fare, the sort of quick-fire stuff the boxing reporters were familiar with. When

Malcolm X, someone not on their beat, chipped in, they were a little disturbed. 'Clay is the finest Negro athlete I have ever known,' he told them, 'the man who will mean more to his people than any athlete before him. He is more than Jackie Robinson was, because Robinson is the white man's hero. The white press wanted him to lose. They wanted him to lose because he is a Muslim. You notice nobody cares about the religion of other athletes. But their prejudice against Clay blinded them to his ability.'

Clay? Even Malcolm X still had not got used to the name switch – partly that was because he was for a day or so Cassius X. It was a time of frantic change and uncertainty in the fighter's life and the sense of chaos would only grow as the years rolled by. Ali thrived on it. He loved confusing reporters as much as he did fighters.

'Black Muslims is a press word,' he told them that day. 'It's not a legitimate name. The real name is Islam. That means peace. Islam is a religion and there are 750 million people all over the world who believe in it, and I'm one of them.' He was right and he was wrong, of course. The Nation of Islam's slice of that number was miniscule. How they wanted it to grow, though.

Ali continued, without pause: 'I ain't no Christian. I can't be, when I see all the coloured people fight for forced integration getting blowed up. They get hit by stones and chewed by dogs, and they blow up a Negro church and don't find the killers. I get telephone calls every day. They want me to carry signs. They want me to picket. They tell me it would be a wonderful thing if I married a white woman because this would be good for brotherhood. I don't want to be blown up. I don't want to be washed down sewers. I just want to be happy with my own kind.'

It was already established that Clay/Ali was no integrationist. The trick was marrying that concept to an understanding that he was not merely a black version of the Ku Klux Klan, who held exactly the same philosophy. For years this troubled the liberal left. How could a member of an oppressed minority hold out against the goodness and fairness of integration? How could Ali sound as if he were some Grand Wizard telling his followers to have nothing to do with those white folks down the road? Ali's critics would point to this anomaly again and again as he resolved the contradiction. It took quite a while.

But there could be no denying the underlying goodness in him. There was love mixed in there with the suspicion. 'People brand us a hate group,' he continued. 'They say we want to take over the country. They say we're Communists. This is not true. Followers of Allah are the sweetest people in the world. They don't carry knives. They don't tote weapons. They pray five times a day. The women wear dresses that come all the way to the floor and they don't commit adultery. All they want to do is live in peace.'

We would learn in the concluding stages of his boxing career how easy adultery came to Ali. For now, his eyes and ears were open only to goodness, to peace and a certain sort of harmony. 'I'm a good boy. I never had done anything wrong. I have never been to jail. I love white people. I like my own people. They can live together without infringing on each other. You can't condemn a man for wanting peace. If you do, you condemn peace itself.' Given his trade, the irony was towering.

A lot of writers didn't want to listen to this stuff. Jimmy Cannon, revered as a leader of his trade, famously wrote: 'The fight racket, since its rotten beginnings, has been the red-light district of sports. But this is the first time it has been turned into an instrument of hate.'

Somehow, Ali's message was not getting through. That stemmed from its fundamental inconsistency of separation and co-habitation, of love and of mistrust. He was parroting a theology patched together by people who'd invented their own mysticism. He believed them without looking too closely. It sounded right to him, like a left hook sunk into the heavy bag. They had nabbed him and he was happy to be nabbed. From this point onwards in his active boxing career he would not betray them or walk away. That disaffection would come later, when he was less prominent, before he re-entered our lives as saint and icon. The cleave was painful but not that public. For now he was a faithful follower of the Nation and of Elijah Muhammad.

Nearly forty years later, I met a man called Truman Gibson. He knew Ali, and Liston too. He knew the latter rather better, as it happens, as well as some of the other lesser-seen people who also knew Liston. Some of them were at that fight in Miami in 1964. I was very interested to hear what he had to say when I went to see him at his attorney's office in the heart of south Chicago. Because Gibson knew where a lot of bodies were buried. Although there were strong rumours of skulduggery surrounding the fight, Gibson doubted they reflected more than the usual movement of wise guys trying to second-guess each other. He was not convinced 'the fix was in', as is the commonly held belief. Suspicions and conspiracy theories are viable currency in boxing, and, certainly, there were more than a few shady geezers in Miami, the Mob's Florida base for several decades. Indeed it was there, at the wretched end of Joe Louis's career in the early 1950s, that Gibson negotiated one more contract for the former heavyweight champion of the world, effectively handing him over to the International Boxing Club run by his friend Jim Norris. But that is another story. What Gibson said about the Clay-Liston fight was informed by that level of inside perspective – and he reckoned it was on the level, even when the world looked agog at their TV screens and saw the unbeatable beast resigned and wrecked on his stool after a truncated performance in which it was widely suspected he had left a stinging substance on his gloves in an effort to blind Clay. Like the bike and the medal, who knew where the truth lay?

One man might, of course. But, as I said, he's not talking much these days ...

Chapter Six
From Shelby to Maine

Now that he had the most prized bauble in sport, the world heavyweight title, Muhammad Ali – as he had become known during the Miami farrago, was, at last, justified in regarding himself as King of the World. It would have the effect, however, of making him more unpopular than any monarch since King John – even though he looked to have rid boxing of its unloved ogre, Sonny Liston.

There would be one last cleansing: the inevitable rematch. Whenever you see an immediate return engagement in boxing, it is as well to suspect something is not quite right. And, although Gibson was sceptical about foul play in Miami, he was less so when the show decamped to the boxing hotbed that is Lewiston, Maine. He had good reason.

Small-town America is a wondrous place. Inasmuch as it exists, it is for purposes of mass appreciation a construct, a perfect, protected world far from the evils of the hurrying world. In the movie version, it is peopled by wholesome folks with hayseed falling from their well-washed hair and wearing do-gooder smiles that suggest they have either swallowed a bible or just arrived from another planet. The reality is a little different, however, to the set of *It's a Wonderful Life*. Small-town America is like New York, with way fewer people but just as many vices. One such pit of idiocy in the grand history of pugilism was Shelby, Montana, whose misfortune it was to have a gullible dreamer called James 'Body' Johnson. The mayor's son was a real-estate agent with access to a telegraphic office, from where he cabled the notorious promoter Doc Kearns in 1923, offering him $200,000 (upped by a third in the end) to bring the great Jack Dempsey to their little mountain community and defend his world heavyweight title against one Tommy Gibbons, who had an excellent record and a penchant for ice cream but was not considered a genuine threat to Dempsey in his prime. However, this fight, reckoned 'Body', would put Shelby on the map. How right he was.

The Doc, Jack and Tommy came to Shelby – a backwater among backwaters with one railway line, no arena, no hotels and no trees. Undaunted, the citizens imported the wood and, in six weeks, built a 40,000-seater stadium and twenty hotels. The ticket prices were hiked so high to recover the investment that only 7,702 people from the surrounding area could afford to pay. Shelby, an oil town in the Rockies with ambitions beyond its resources, home to just a few thousand innocent souls and a stupid mayor's son, went broke. Four local banks closed. Doc and the fighters skipped town, although it is said Mr Gibbons didn't get much for his bruises, while Kearns and Dempsey rolled on to bigger and richer glories.

Lewiston, Maine, was not quite as strategically isolated as Shelby, Montana, but they had much in common: small, unknown, willing to please and dangerously green in the ways of the boxing business. They each would host just the one world heavyweight title, and be glad not to go through the experience twice. Lewiston had a population of about 30,000 but, as in Shelby, only a small slice of the residents bothered to attend when Muhammad Ali and Sonny Liston rolled into town.

The fight took place fifteen months to the day after the pair had first met in the ring and the venue, St Dominic's Hall, was not exactly bursting in accommodating 2,434 fans, a third of the number who watched the champion's professional debut five years earlier in the Freedom Hall in the fairground in

Louisville – and about a tenth of the population of Lewiston. How did this come to be?

This is a part of the narrative where Ali and his supposedly whiter-than-white white backers got to learn how the boxing business really works. This was their Doc Kearns moment. Every single thing about this fight was farcical, from setting it up to the finishing punch. It should be included in any FBI manual on how to spot a scam. Nobody has ever been charged, convicted or even questioned about this hilarious episode in Ali's life, but it is worth recounting the skeletal details, because they reflect poorly on everyone involved, including the man himself.

It stretches back to Cus D'Amato, often portrayed since his death as a sainted figure, railing against injustice and, sleeping with a gun under his pillow, surviving battles with the Mob who ran boxing in the 1950s, something of a touchstone for goodness. It was not quite like that, as with so many things in the fight business.

When D'Amato had Patterson as champ – inaccurately described by the normally spot-on Red Smith of *The New York Times* as 'the man of peace who loves to fight' – he resisted all attempts to match him with the obvious challenger, Liston. Forced to do so when the champion's position was becoming more untenable by the day, he negotiated a clause for an immediate rematch if his man lost – which he knew he would. They had another fight, made more money, and Patterson was pushed from the picture for a good few years, handing the crown to the biggest villain in the sport, Charles Sonny Liston.

As a result of breaking all regulations and doing a deal for a rematch, D'Amato unwittingly forced the hand of the major governing body of the time, the World Boxing Association, which subsequently threatened sanctions against any champion who tried to pull that little number again. Which brings us to Lewiston, Maine – via Boston, Massachusetts, as it happens, because that is where the second Ali-Liston fight was supposed to happen.

With the WBA now threatening to suspend any member state who staged an illegal rematch, there were two developments, perhaps not entirely unconnected. The WBA suspended the Massachusetts affiliated body and Ali developed a hernia three days before the scheduled fight, at the Boston Garden on 16 November 1964.

Postponed to 25 May the following year, the fixture remained dogged by doubt. The Suffolk County District Attorney Garrett Byrne, in whose jurisdiction the planned bout would take place, had heard rumours of organised crime involvement, hardly a shock given Liston's background, managed at various stages by a string of hoodlums connected to the sport's 1950s godfathers, Blinky Palermo and Frankie Carbo – business partners of Norris and Gibson, if you can follow that spiderweb of intrigue.

The particular organisation in question, Inter-Continental Promotions (chief executive, Robert Nilon, whose brother Jack was one of Liston's many managers), denied it was their show; as well they might, given their reason for existing was to promote Liston's fights – as well as the right to promote Ali's first fight as champion, and pick his opponent. No, said Inter-Continental, the real promoter was the hitherto little-mentioned Sam Silverman, who promoted most of Rocky Marciano's fights and knew every mobster in New England.

So Inter-Continental and all their friends got booted out of the state, which is how Ali and Liston ended up in an echoing hall on 25 May 1965, in Lewiston, Maine, previously best known for a few mills and lots of churches in a pleasant setting. It was not fight central. There were more than 1,500 empty seats on the town's big night, ensuring its place in boxing history for the lowest attendance at any world heavyweight title fight – just a few more than saw Dempsey and Gibbons duke it out in Shelby, forty-one years earlier.

Ali-Liston II lived down to the billing. This was the night of the phantom punch – allegedly. The judgment is not quite fair. Ali did land a tough-to-see, wickedly short right to Liston's jaw in the first round and down went Sonny, who did his best to stay down while the referee, the former champ Jersey Joe Walcott, made a mess of the count. One of the ringside judges, incidentally, was the former heavyweight Coley Wallace, better known as Joe Louis's regular sparring partner and who would go on to play Joe in a biopic. Boxing is a tight-knit family, indeed.

When Sonny did rise, he did not look in the worst shape of his life, but he did look relieved. Ali told his biographer Thomas Hauser: 'The punch jarred him. It was a good punch, but I didn't think I hit him so hard he couldn't get up.'

There were more opinions in the aftermath than there were predictions before it. Among the most interesting account years later was the one Mark Kram alleged Liston gave to him for the readers of *Sports Illustrated*: 'That guy was crazy. I didn't want anything to do with him. And the Muslims were coming up. Who needed that? So I went down. I wasn't hit.'

Liston told someone else he didn't even hear a count, so he didn't get up, but he could have. His wife, Geraldine, revealed years later that Liston told her when he got home that he reckoned it was as well to get paid the same money for a one-round whooping as over the full course. However, thirty years later, a former FBI agent, William Roemer, claimed in a documentary on HBO that a mobbed-up Chicago boxing manager called Bernie Glickman told him he had heard Geraldine tell Liston before the fight that going down early and staying there probably was his best choice that evening.

And years later I asked Al Certo, Liston's friend, what he thought. 'He was a killer,' Certo said, unemotionally. 'Probably his hands were tied in that fight. It was a tank job.'

One way or another, the quick and otherwise spectacular victory did Ali a lot of damage. The mainstream fight media, and their clever cohorts on the fancy comment pages, already disliked him intensely, with few exceptions. They only needed an excuse to stick their daggers further into his gullet and there were immediate whispers that the Nation of Islam, whom they neither knew nor understood and who had co-opted Clay to their number as Muhammad Ali during and after the first controversial fight, were now tightening their mysterious grip around his throat and the whole sport of boxing.

Liston said so. For maybe the only time in his life, the media guys believed him.

It was not quite so that the Nation wanted to run boxing, as tempting a thought as that might have been to the conspiracy theorists. But they were undeniably now in the boxing business. Their man had the title. If it was a sport that hardly raised a pious eyebrow previously among their disciples, everybody clamoured now for a piece of Ali. And right there at the head of the queue was Elijah Muhammad, the religion's ego-maniacal leader who had pretty much total control of the organisation and who held Ali in his charismatic embrace. Ali hung on Elijah's every word. He believed every single sentence that fell from the great man's blessed lips. There was no room for doubt or argument. Ali, always sure of his destiny in the ring, now saw a vision wide and more glorious than that, the one sold him by the Nation of Islam and its dictatorial leader.

Ali, raised a Baptist, had always been unusually respectful of people in authority, whatever his image of rebellion as he grew into his public persona. And the way he spoke of Elijah Muhammad was significantly at odds with the way he spoke about opponents, for instance. He was now a holy man away from the ring but still a beast within the ropes, still taunting, poking, humiliating – all the sins you would imagine a righteous man would find abhorrent.

This was the period when some of the contradictions that would come to define the complex character of Muhammad Ali began to coalesce. He was never easy to understand before this time; now he would become a chess conundrum of Boris Spassky proportions.

What is remarkable about this first storm of many is how easily Ali handled it. He did not even appear to get his hair wet as waves of derision crashed down on him. There were all sorts of repercussions likely, or at least possible, after they had laughed in the face of the WBA. Such intransigence by the ruling bodies and matching disobedience by Ali and the Nation would set a pattern for recurring anarchy for the rest of his boxing career. It seemed not to bother him a jot.

The fight writers couldn't pin a fix on Ali-Liston II, but the rest of the world pretty much did it for them. It was impossible to find anyone who believed that Ali had legitimately knocked out Liston. Even I doubted it when, finally, some footage reached Maitland, probably weeks later on TV. I kept the faith, mind. Nobody was budging me from believing in Cassius Clay, whatever his name was now. He was still The Greatest. He'd told us he was – he had to be.

Chapter Seven
Writers Not Fighters

Nowhere in sport is the connection between participants and observers as tenuous as it is in boxing. Most football writers played football. Ditto cricket and rugby. Those are sports in which it is possible to be mediocre and not killed. Some writers and commentators gloved up in their youth – a few did so seriously, but, increasingly, those numbers have dwindled. This does not mean there have not been wonderful fight writers who didn't box. Two of the very best in my lifetime have been Harry Mullan and Hugh McIlvanney, neither of whom, by their own admission, did more than dabble in the gym when young.

There's fighting and there's fighting, however. Go back a generation or two and a lot of young men who ended up in journalism and its many offshoots through circuitous routes had fought for real, in the war.

The American sportswriting fraternity is a curious collection of talents and egos, invested with much self-appointed gravitas, some of it warranted, much of it not. And there has long been – as elsewhere in the world – an element of the avalanche journalism that has a life of its own. If one serious boxing writer pronounces, you can be pretty sure so will his rivals. Or that, at least, is the way it used to be.

Bert Sugar, sadly no longer with us, grew up in the business in the 1950s and 1960s, and nailed the trade with perfect irreverence. 'I used to call the old writers Sir Lunchalots,' he told me over umpteen beers in Manhattan one fight night near Madison Square Garden (the fourth one). 'They'd all have their envelopes from the Garden, their pay-offs. They'd take home doggy bags, through snowstorms. They hadn't eaten in months some of those guys. But they knew what was going on. They knew the fixed fights.' At least they said they did.

The most influential boxing commentator of the day was not one of the Sir Lunchalots. But he was, by his own admission, the most pompous: Howard Cosell, the voice of boxing on ABC TV. He wore an impossible-to-miss hairpiece and a naff yellow blazer, spoke in that sombre way borne of staggering self-importance and he formed a relationship with Muhammad Ali that was as much an entertaining double act as was that of, many years later, Harry Carpenter and Frank Bruno. It served Cosell and Ali's purposes, as extroverts, to make the most of this odd union: the university-educated wise guy and the Louisville lunatic. That is how the world saw them: such opposites they were bound to attract each other.

In shaping the public's perception of Ali, Cosell would define his own career (like so many) that otherwise would have been regarded as routinely successful. Ali made Cosell; contrary to what this absurd but talented egotist might have sometimes imagined, Cosell did not make Ali. It is a common failing among journalists who reach a certain eminence to think that they have more influence and significance than they actually do in the discovery and encouragement of legends.

Certainly, Ali breathed hard and often from the lung of publicity; it was, indeed, his primary juice outside the adrenaline rush he obtained from embarrassing opponents in the ring. But he generated most of that heat himself. There was no evil genius writing his script. He needed no publicist, as such. He was a walking, never-stop-talking gift to the show business of sport, to every reporter he ever came in contact with – all of whom, without any shadow of a doubt, will have considered themselves somehow part of Ali's life, however brief or inconsequential their brush of his cloak. I will come to my own little sentence in his story later. For now, let us look back at the writers and commentators, mainly in his own country, who did have a say in the making of Ali, but probably not in the way they recall. What a lot of them did, in many ways, was a travesty: falling in behind the Establishment view that this gentle, funny, crazy guy with the big mouth was somehow a threat to the fabric of their great democracy. If only they had looked a little deeper (which many of them did, but way too late), they would have seen where the real villains lurked.

Some of the best stuff written about the fight game arrived before most of us were born. And I have always taken comfort in relying on John Lardner (son of Ring Lardner and beneficiary of a childhood spent in the company of such literary behemoths as F. Scott Fitzgerald and Dorothy Parker) for wisdom that has seemed reliable through the decades. 'A curious thing about boxing,' Lardner wrote in *White Hopes and Other Tigers* in 1951, 'is that most matches, considered intrinsically as athletic events, are interesting only to seasoned experts and fans. The crowd at large is concerned with the issues behind them, and the flavour of the characters involved. Each big prizefight is a climax in a story, or series of stories, about people. The fight game has a way of overlapping into many of the lively social arts of man: politics, drinking, litigation, the stage, the motion pictures, popular fiction, larceny and propaganda. That side of it, the byplay, is what appeals most to me.'

Well said, Mr Lardner. I suspect Mr Cosell, for all his bombast, shared those sentiments. Cosell was the grandson of a rabbi, born in North Carolina in 1918, fashioned in Brooklyn, educated in English and law at two New York universities. He went to war, came home, got married and grew up in the East Coast liberal Jewish tradition of that space and time, moving from a legal career to radio broadcasting in the 1950s. However, he brought something extra to his commentaries, not least a memorable broadcasting voice, stopping for emphasis at nearly every word, rolling each around his tongue as if it were a favourite sweet. He was aware of it, of that there could be no doubt. It set him apart from his contemporaries, who probably fumed that this often obnoxious man was getting all the big gigs, from the Friday night football to the boxing.

Unable to resist the temptation to intellectualise, Cosell personalised his journalism, setting a new tone and standard – not always liked, but never ignored – and it was almost inevitable that such an opinionated commentator would be picked up sooner or later by television and just as certain that he would one day collide with the biggest name in sport, Muhammad Ali. For sixteen years, they jousted on ABC, free to air, making Cosell not just a significant part of the story but internationally famous, a willing straight man to Ali's clowning persona. It worked brilliantly, and they both loved it.

But, for all the laughs – and there were many – one episode defined their relationship. It took courage for Cosell to stand up for Ali when everyone else was running for cover, when a nation unsure of itself in war in faraway Vietnam did not know what to think of their heavyweight champion for refusing to fight. What right did Ali have, this megaphone black man who'd changed his name and espoused this strange religion, what right did he have to exclude himself from his duty? There was real and deep hostility towards him when he refused the draft. And one of the very few friends he had in the media at that time was the pompous man in the ridiculous toupee.

Chapter Eight
A Different Kind of Fight

After beating Liston a second time, Ali embarked on a quite stunning string of defences. They came, they peered beyond those magic gloves, they fell. He was, quite simply, glorious. He looked invincible. He looked beautiful. He looked as if he could be the champion of the world forever. Muhammad Ali was, simply, The Greatest – just like he told us.

He was cruel to Floyd Patterson, carrying him way longer than he needed to, twelve of the scheduled fifteen rounds, before despatching him – punishment for daring to side with white America, to question his religion, to even imagine he was worth a place in the same ring. On the last count, at least, he was right. Patterson, flickering brilliant himself as a small but lightning-quick heavyweight, was a shell when he stepped up against Ali at the Convention Center in Las Vegas in November 1965.

Patterson would knock out Henry Cooper the following September in London, but he was spent as a force at the highest level, wrecked first by Liston and finished off by Ali – whom he insisted on calling Clay (when Ali gave him one more chance, beating him into submission in seven rounds in 1972, he would finally acquiesce). Deigning not to address Ali by his chosen name was a mistake another fighter would make – and pay for.

George Chuvalo at least stayed on his feet for fifteen rounds in March of 1966; Cooper's tissue-like skin let him down again two months after that in their second fight, when Ali returned to the UK and was bedazzled by the spectacle of England winning the World Cup at Wembley. He was less impressed by Brian London, who timidly succumbed in three rounds at Earls Court, three months later.

On his European tour, he stopped off in Frankfurt in September to take care of Karl Mildenberger. It created minor sports history: the first sporting event broadcast via satellite in colour – much good it did the German, the first German since Max Schmeling to challenge for the world title. He lost in the twelfth – and Ali found a new audience in Germany. He was still not totally accepted at home, but they loved him in Europe. How long would it last?

Ali was now consumed by other difficulties, however. He had decided, on the advice of Elijah Muhammad and other leaders in the Nation of Islam, to refuse military service in Vietnam, where the conflict had stumbled towards an ugly denouement. America was stunned. The heavyweight champion of the world was declining to stand by the flag. But he would not budge. He claimed he was a practising Muslim minister and, on religious grounds, entitled to be absented from the obligation to kill in the name of his country.

In the ring, Ali looked as if he were replicating Joe Louis's 'Bum of the Month' routine — although greater hopes were held for the chances of Cleveland 'Big Cat' Williams at the Astrodome in Houston just before Christmas. However, all Big Cat could do was provide Ali with a target on which to display his now near-perfect boxing skills. It was a sublime performance. Williams, a veteran of seventy-one fights, sixty-five of them wins, was rendered impotent in the face of the champion's whirring gloves in the three rounds it lasted.

Always able to juggle multiple challenges, Ali let the Nation's lawyers — and those members of the liberal media who had come to see his objection to fighting as a *cause célèbre* in the context of a dirty, pointless war — deal with his legal problem and continued to blossom as a fighter. He took particular delight in humiliating his next opponent. Back in the Astrodome, he fought a man with as little respect for his new religion as Patterson had shown: Ernie Terrell. But, whereas Patterson was almost meek in his refusal to call him Ali, Terrell spoke more firmly: there was fire in his belly. He seemed more determined than the others to stop the Ali train – and he was not going to bow before the champion. He would call him Clay. What a mistake he made.

From the first round, Ali hit his tough and competent challenger with such a blizzard of leather that Terrell hardly knew where to look. He'd come to the fight with a respectable record. He'd beaten such fine fighters as Cleveland Williams, Zora Folley, Bob Foster, Eddie Machen, George Chuvalo and Doug Jones, six excellent victories among thirty-nine in forty-three bouts. But none of them prepared him for what he had to endure that night in front of 37,000 shocked Texans. He earned every cent of his $210,000 purse as Ali used him as a punchbag for fifteen rounds when – as against Patterson – he could have finished the ordeal much earlier. In the eighth round he unleashed his ultimate spear: 'What's my name?' he inquired of Terrell. 'What's my name?' Over and over again, he demanded that he pay homage. 'What's my name?' You could just hear it on the TV broadcast. Around the world, fight fans witnessed a champion humiliate a challenger as if he were bullying a child in the playground. It was to have a profound effect on Ali's image, which was already on the rocks.

Alone among black fighters, Ali had no compunction about using language that was usually off limits. He'd called Patterson an Uncle Tom and he called Terrell an Uncle Tom. Neither was that; both were decent men. In later years, both would forgive Ali for this terrible slight. But he did not hold back in his tirades – and, whatever he might say – he could not attribute it all to the selling of tickets. A good part of his act sprung from a genuine resentment that he was not joined in his ideological fight against white America by his black brothers. He was, he reckoned, doing it all on his own. This was a significant skewing of the facts. He certainly was adamant in his views – but so were several other black athletes of his time. And was it up to him to judge who should and should not be respected in the black community on the strength or otherwise of their protest? He thought so. Certainly, the Nation of Islam thought so. They encouraged Ali at every turn to spout their views, and those views were not always comfortable ones.

Consistently and constantly, he spoke about the 'blue-eyed devils' even to those friends in the liberal white community who were in the vanguard of civil rights, who wanted the status quo to change, who wanted white America to bend to the growing call for genuine equality rather than the cardboard version that existed. But too often Ali was deaf to this help. He seemed to be driven by another voice, offstage. He gave every impression of being not so much the instigator of his own thoughts but a puppet on a string. And, when he heard those sorts of whispers, the heavyweight champion of the world did not like it one bit. It only strengthened his view that white America remained his implacable enemy and any of his black brothers and sisters who did not agree with him were also his enemy. There could be no doubting his stubbornness.

Victory over Terrell returned to him the WBA title that had been taken away when he defied the organisation back in 1965 for giving Liston a rematch. Now, he reckoned, he had tamed his inquisitors. Now he really was on top of the world. They could question his supremacy no more. There was a strut in Ali's step to go with the growing excellence of his boxing. Not everyone appreciated this development. Even I wondered, occasionally. I was in high school, still, and imagining that in a couple of years I would have to go out and earn a living – or maybe fight in Vietnam.

For those who criticise Ali's refusal to fight in Vietnam, some perspective might be useful. In my case, it was the real possibility of going off to a very much fractured warzone at the end of my high school days. I finished school in 1969, aged nineteen, having started late for a variety of reasons. I turned twenty on 24 December that year. It was, we were informed, the last draft and, promised the politicians, no conscripts would go to Vietnam. Part of me was disappointed – I wanted an adventure. The rest of me was terrified. A couple of friends had already gone, including a cousin, and they'd seen some horrific things, strung-out young American GIs wandering the brothels of Saigon, losing their brains, their identity and their will to fight as rumour after rumour of another Viet Cong onslaught buzzed the southern capital. It was, my friends said, anarchy. 'You don't want to go near that place.'

As it happened, I didn't. Using a system introduced in 1964, draftees were selected in a random selection of birthdays: six from the first six months of the year, and six from the second. Three of the dates that came up in my half of 1969 landed in December – all of them within a couple of days of my birthday, Christmas Eve. It was as if I had literally dodged a bullet. A couple more schoolmates went, though – despite the promises they would be held at home, and they saw plenty of grim stuff as the war descended into the most awful mess. The end of a war is worse than the beginning, because it is then where death becomes increasingly pointless, as another armistice or ceasefire is arranged by old men safely cosseted in a grand hotel in Paris, far from the shooting. To die on the last day of a war was the very more serious version of being knocked out in the last round.

Thankful, then, that I did not get to experience the thrill of risking death in battle, I set about getting a job. How I wanted to be a sportswriter. How I wanted to write about boxing, about Muhammad Ali. But what would become of my hero? He was straying dangerously into a different, heavy line of fire. He had somehow won over a section of fans after his crazy win over Liston in Miami and impressed aficionados with his sublime and very different boxing skills, but the mood seemed to be shifting again as his career moved towards its zenith. White America again struggled to cope with his arrogance, his aloofness, his lack of patriotism. And they certainly did not like those guys in the funny hats, the ones who you'd always seen on the edge, scowling, arms folded.

There was a rumbling sentiment around this time that Ali's private and public lives could no longer be kept separate. He would have to deal with his toughest foe to date: the United States government.

And here we come to another intriguing twist: just as Ali was becoming increasingly demonised, the debate would descend into a forest of complicated morality. How he cut his way through that forest would determine his legacy. But, in the beginning, it did not look good for the man many people still chose to call Cassius Clay.

Among those so disposed were the unsmiling, crew-cut gentlemen of the draft board. These were not obviously free-thinking individuals. They showed no sign of life behind their steely eyes, gave no hint that they spoke for themselves. And that was their shield. They could say only what they were constitutionally obligated to say. The same applied to those members of the legal system, the judges and well-paid attorneys who would become embroiled in one of the most fascinating and significant cases of 1960s America, as it wrestled with the moral dilemma of Vietnam: to wave the flag in a lost cause, but wave it nonetheless. Not to shoot a gun on behalf of the United States of America – however wrongheaded the cause – was, in the eyes of a vast number of citizens, to commit the ultimate sin. To be unpatriotic in America, the most patriotic country on the planet, was unforgiveable. And Muhammad Ali most definitely was not looking for forgiveness – or even understanding. He had reached a stage of intransigence that went beyond negotiation. In a way that was his strength. He paid no heed to the legitimacy of the counter arguments. He had total faith in his own case. He knew he was right and that righteousness, he said, would conquer all argument.

Before we look at how Muhammad Ali came to sacrifice a significant chunk of his career – at the very time when he was at his athletic peak – it is instructive to examine some of his inspiration. As mentioned earlier, the young Cassius Clay had wanted first Joe Louis then Sugar Ray Robinson, the two greatest black fighters in the history of boxing, to guide his career, and was disappointed when, for a variety of reasons, they rejected him. He always suspected their underlying objection to him was not as a boxer but as a rebellious spirit, someone they might struggle to tame, just as nobody really could tame Jack Johnson. Because it is Jack Johnson who really inspired Muhammad Ali – more so even than Elijah Muhammad or any of his Nation lackeys.

Jack Johnson was a remarkable man. Not just because he was the heavyweight champion of the world, and the first black man to own the title –

although those are the reasons we know of his greatness – but Johnson's true genius lay elsewhere. Had he not been a professional boxer, he might have been a politician, a lawyer, an entertainer in another, less dangerous corner of show business, perhaps. Some say he would probably have run a high-class bordello. Some say that is probably what he was doing, anyway. Or he might have been dead before his story properly began.

Johnson lived in Texas, born in Galveston in 1878 to parents only removed by a single generation from slavery. He was there when a hurricane ripped the city open like a can of beans, and also when a storm of biblical strength roared at 145 miles per hour through that unstable region in 1900, killing an estimated 8,000 people and wiping out whole towns. Jack survived both nightmares – as he nearly always did.

Converting his strength to dollars was a simple process. He fought for a living, became pretty much unbeatable and, therefore, unmatchable. Nobody wanted to fight a black man except other black men. And nobody wanted to fight a black man as good as Jack Johnson, black or white. But he chased the champ, the under-sized Tommy Burns, all the way to Sydney in 1908 and beat the hell out of him, the constabulary entering the ring to save the white man extended pain and indignity. Jack London, the author, was there – and he created a myth when he called for a 'great white hope' to unseat this leering champion with 'the golden smile'. It was a crusade that would blight boxing and society for decades. Jack? He wasn't bothered.

In Reno, Nevada, on 4 July 1910, Johnson, now peerless among heavyweights and smiling his golden smile throughout, fought the recalled 'great white hope' James J. Jeffries, and beat the poor man to a pulp in front of a shocked white audience, before law enforcement officers – again – entered the ring to stop the slaughter, and turn off the cameras.

What happened in the wake of that fight was not just a disgrace and a scandal: it was – or should have been – a matter of national shame for a country built on the rights of oppressed people. Riots and lynchings terrorised black Americans. Estimates vary, but at least twenty innocent black men were publicly hanged, stabbed or shot, without retribution, for no reason other than they shared the skin colour of the man who had humiliated a reluctant and old white challenger in Nevada. What sparked much of this outrage was the existence of film footage of the fight. Wherever it was shown, it caused a storm. Just as Ali's notoriety spread through the very medium he would come to dominate, so

Johnson's win was used against him and other black Americans because of the moving images of the fight.

There was also a ballad written, a black ballad, reproduced in the *Omaha Daily News* on 9 July 1910, more popular in southern cotton fields and Harlem, no doubt, than on Wall Street:

> *Amaze an' Grace, how sweet it sounds,*
> *Jack Johnson knocked Jim Jeffries down.*
> *Jim Jeffries jumped up an' hit Jack on the chin,*
> *An' then Jack knocked him down again.*
> *The Yankees hold the play,*
> *The White man pull the trigger;*
> *But it makes no difference what the white man say;*
> *The world champion's still a nigger.*

'Still a nigger'. I have heard Ali say that many times. Only when I read about the Johnson-Jeffries fight and came across those lyrics did I make the connection with his past, and appreciate the length and depth of the struggle. It was a phrase that sprung from deep in his DNA, something he just knew and embraced. 'Still a nigger': what a powerful uppercut of pride that is.

And, as Johnson wrote years later, 'Prejudices were being piled up against me and, certain unfair persons, piqued because I was champion decided that [if] they could not get me one way they would another.'

The other way was the Mann Act, enacted in 1908, which barred the 'transportation of women in interstate or foreign congress for the purpose of prostitution or debauchery or any other immoral purpose'. Its shorthand reference was 'the white slave act', an irony lost on most in this case.

The Justice Department seized on it to enslave Johnson – in October 1912, through his association with a nineteen-year-old prostitute called Lucille Cameron. Her mother went to the Chicago police claiming the fighter had abducted her daughter. 'Jack Johnson has hypnotic powers,' she told Chicago journalists, 'and yet exercised them on my little girl. I would rather see my daughter spend the rest of her life in an insane asylum than see her the plaything of a nigger.'

The authorities blatantly abused the Mann Act – which was not designed for 'individual liaisons' – and arrested Johnson. It was not so much that Johnson held the world heavyweight title that angered these angels of vengeance; it was that he was having a relationship with a white woman – indeed, several white women over a long period of time. Just as he laughed at Jeffries in the ring, so he was perceived to be laughing at white America outside of it. They were going to knock him out.

Within days, Chicago's burghers had closed Johnson's Café de Champion nightclub. Johnson's response was clear and simple: 'I am not a slave and I have the right to chose who my mate shall be, without the dictation of any man. I have eyes and I have a heart and when they fail to tell me who I shall have as mine, I want to be put in a lunatic asylum.'

How Ali's words more than fifty years later would so eerily echo Johnson's sentiment, when he told reporters after beating Liston to win the title: 'I don't have to be who you want me to be.' That, essentially, was the crux of the issue: self-determination, a person's right to be who he or she wants to be: black, white, gay, straight, left, right, fat, fit, smart, dumb, ugly, beautiful – all the myriad interpretations of those classifications.

Lucille Cameron saved Johnson, refusing to testify against him, and the case collapsed. But they were not done with the champion yet – and they had public sentiment with them.

What happened to Johnson thereafter was analogous with what would befall Ali in his long legal fight with the Establishment. Agents went to extraordinary lengths across the country to get dirt on Johnson. It wasn't hard to find. He did not live what his contemporaries would regard as a saintly existence. There is a delightful novel, based roughly on facts, that describes the rabble-rousing escapades of Johnson and the white fighter he knocked unconscious, Stanley Ketchel, after being put down himself. They were both outsiders, Jack and Stanley, and in *The Killings of Stanley Ketchel: A Novel*, the author, James Carlos Blake, paints a vivid picture of rolling debauchery across America, as the two fighters rumble from one brothel to the next, fighting, drinking, gambling and whoring their money away.

The authorities, meanwhile, found Belle Schreiber, Jack's aggrieved ex-lover of four years, who was working in a brothel in Washington. She testified he had taken her from Pittsburgh to Chicago in August 1910 'for the purposes of prostitution and debauchery'. They arrested him in November. The judge on the bench was one Kenesaw Mountain Landis. He would later be baseball's commissioner, and ensure the sport remained segregated until Jack Roosevelt 'Jackie' Robinson broke the chains and stepped out for the Brooklyn Dodgers on 15 April 1947. Landis put Johnson in jail, refusing his bail application. Ali knew that history – it was seared into his consciousness.

Johnson did get out – and married Cameron in December 1912. This was a spear to the heart of white supremacists – miscegenation, as it was called – that reached back to the days of the lauded Thomas Jefferson, a slave-owner written into history as a man of democracy and liberation. It took an all-white jury two hours to find Johnson guilty of contravening the Mann Act, even though the charges related to incidents before its implementation.

As the American film-maker Ken Burns, quoting the revered African-American academic W.E.B. Du Bois, Johnson suffered because of his 'unforgivable blackness'.

On 4 June 1913, Johnson was sentenced to a year and a day. He was free, pending an appeal – so he skipped town. Skipped the country, in fact. And what an escape it was: disguised among other black athletes, the members of a baseball team, he went north to Canada. His mother said he bribed the Feds, but nothing was proved. On 25 June, he arrived in Montreal, to be met by Lucille. They fled to Europe.

On earlier trips to Europe, he had been feted as an exotic celebrity. Not now. Hotel doors closed in Paris, likewise in London. Sweden would not let him in at all. He went back to the ring, and on 28 June 1914 he fought the white American Frank

Moran in Paris. It was a farcical exhibition, as if that mattered. That very afternoon Archduke Franz Ferdinand was assassinated in Sarajevo and the world would soon be hurled into the First World War. Jack waged his own war.

D.W. Griffiths' film *Birth of a Nation*, a glorification of white supremacy, excited cinema audiences across America – after a screening at the White House celebrated by Woodrow Wilson. Ali knew this history, too.

On 5 April 1915, Kansas ranch hand Jess Willard – at 6ft 6in, 250 lbs, a giant of his day – who did not box until he was twenty-seven (ten years younger than Jack) stepped up as the next 'great white hope' that Jack London had been calling for since Johnson took the title from poor Tommy Burns in faraway Sydney, seven years earlier. Jeffries had proved inadequate. And, while Willard didn't much like fighting and certainly was not as good a practitioner as Jeffries, he was big and he could hit. The champion nobody wanted would get $35,000 and an unconfirmed promise to have the charges against him dropped. At the racetrack in Havana, Cuba, Willard knocked Johnson out in the twenty-sixth round – and it would be fifteen years before another black man, Joe Louis, was allowed to fight for the heavyweight title again.

Johnson, meanwhile, went to England, got in a fight, and had to leave the country. From there he went to Spain, from where he volunteered to fight with the US Armed Forces when they came to the Great War in France in 1917, but he was refused. The pattern of rejection, something to which he had long been accustomed, continued. Is it any wonder he developed such a tough skin and a thin-eyed view of white society? And what an irony that the fighter with whom Ali most identified had volunteered to go to war.

The government banned Johnson from his mother's funeral. He drank and went broke, but he was still with Lucille. They went to Mexico, where he was lauded. In 1920, Johnson again asked the US government if he could come home and do his time. They agreed. It may have been the scene of his persecution, but America was home. On 20 July 1920, Johnson crossed the US border at Tijuana and gave himself up. He served his term at Fort Leavenworth, Kansas, and, en route, crowds everywhere greeted his train when it stopped. Jack was still a celebrity, whatever white America said, and, true to his sense of style, he drove himself into prison in a borrowed car. Discharged on 9 July 1921, he was met by still-loyal Lucille, and mobbed at the gates. He was forty-three. Had the

Establishment finally got rid of their troublesome black irritant? Not altogether.

Jack, flabby and dissolute now, called for a fight with Dempsey, the champion who had dethroned Willard, but was ignored. Johnson then fought in Canada and Cuba in meaningless bouts before returning to vaudeville to cash in on his own ever-more pathetic image. He tried acting; he ran a Harlem nightclub, which the Leeds-born gangster Owney Madden bought and turned into the subsequently famous Cotton Club, entertaining every mobster in town, as well as leading members of the fight fraternity. In 1924 Lucille divorced Johnson on grounds of infidelity. He remarried the following year. In 1936, he backed New Dealer Franklin D. Roosevelt in the nation's elections and seemed to have inveigled his way back into the mainstream.

Then Joe Louis arrived, and Johnson was not pleased with his compliant attitude to the still-overwhelming white boxing Establishment. Yet, ever the astute opportunist, he offered to be his trainer before the first Max Schmeling fight in 1936. Louis's black management refused, and Johnson declared the German would win, which he did.

Thereafter, Johnson's life was reduced to appearances in small nightclubs around New York.

It ended farcically. Driving back towards New York at high speed from Raleigh, North Carolina, on 10 June 1946, he crashed along Highway 1. Johnson died in hospital a few hours later, aged sixty-eight. He was on his way to watch a fight in New York: Joe Louis vs Billy Conn.

Johnson's excellent biographer, Randy Roberts, concluded in *Papa Jack: Jack Johnson and the Era of White Hopes*: 'Taken as a whole, his life inspires respect. He faced a sea of white hate without fear. He refused to consider himself a second-class citizen and wrote the rules for his own life. But the self-centredness that allowed him to do these things left most observers cold. It is only from a safe distance, intellectual as well as physical, that Jack Johnson could honestly be admired as a man'.

It sounds a harsh judgment and is not entirely without merit. But Johnson was very much a product of his time. His boxing prowess gave him the one way available to be who he wanted to be. And who he was did not conform to any image of sainthood. Roberts has a problem with that; Jack, certainly, did not.

'I was a brunette in a blonde town,' Jack once said, 'but, gentlemen, I did not stop stepping.'

And Muhammad Ali did not 'stop stepping'. He would not be silenced. He would not bow to the authorities because he no longer gave credence to the law of the land. This was the ultimate act or rebellion, not dissimilar to Johnson's strong-minded reaction to authority at every turn. It sprang from a deep conviction, however misguided many of his friends thought he might be in consorting with the Nation, and signing up to their warped agenda.

This, then, brings us to half-time in Ali's story. This is the turning point. It is here where the remaking of Ali begins, not altogether seamlessly, but with so much drama that his fight for freedom and self-determination away from the ring was every bit as absorbing as those boxing matches that put him centre stage in the first place. Had Muhammad Ali been not much good at boxing, of course, we would never have heard about him. It was his fighting talent that propelled him into the eye of a different hurricane, one of words and principals rather than blood and bruises. He would prove every bit as obdurate and difficult to hit in a suit as in a pair of shorts.

For all that Richard Durham's ghosting of Ali's story is widely regarded as slanted, because of his association with the Nation of Islam, there is no reason to doubt his version of events during that period. The events in question began to bubble up in 1966, when the fighter initially refused military service, and properly got under way on 28 April 1967, when the US Justice Department denied his claim, insisting his refusal to serve was based on political rather than religious grounds. They upgraded his status from 1-Y, which would have given him a pass on academic grounds, to 1-A, which meant he was fit in every way to go to war.

So, in Ali's ghosted words, this is how he famously responded: 'I had come out into the front yard of the little gray cement cottage that my White South Christian Millionaire Sponsors had rented in my name in the black section of Miami. A TV report had been set up to ask my reaction … I gave it: "I ain't got no quarrel with the Viet Cong." Later, when they kept asking the same question, I rhymed it for them:

> *"Keep asking me, no matter how long,*
> *On the war in Vietnam, I sing this song,*
> *I ain't got no quarrel with the Viet Cong …"'*

The white media were, with few exceptions, merciless in their condemnation of Ali. It was as if the entire force of the American Establishment was lined up against Ali, in a manner that was too reminiscent of the way Johnson had been treated from the moment he won the title until his death.

He'd struggled to find a venue to fight Ernie Terrell, the fight coming after he'd made clear his views on Vietnam. Afterwards, it got heavy. Jim Murray, of *The Los Angeles Times*, now described Ali as 'black Benedict Arnold'. He advised him, 'not to go near the statue of Lincoln. Those will be real tears running down his cheeks'.

Others chimed in, viciously. The *Toronto Star* ran a headline that read: 'Clay is Hated by Millions'. Some claim Jack Dempsey declared Ali was, 'finished as a fighter'.

Durham has Ali saying in response: 'It was as though I had touched an electric switch that let loose the pent-up hatred and bitterness that a big section of white America had long wanted to unleash on me for all my cockiness and boasting, for declaring myself The Greatest without waiting for their kind approval. For branding their Christianity a farce and flaunting my own religion, for preaching, among my own people without apology, a "black is best" philosophy. For frustrating their desire to see me whipped "for the good of the country" and joyfully marching off to the bank with the fruits of it and setting them up to try again. In the days ahead, the same people who found me a "fresh breeze to boxing", who had found my poetry "humorous" and my quips "funny", would agree with Bill Gleason of the [*Chicago*] *Sun-Times* that, "He isn't funny, he's tragic", or, as one writer put it, "dangerous for the youth of America".'

This was always an underlying theme: the threat to the fabric of America's values and culture, with nobody more vulnerable than the Americans of tomorrow, the youth who needed guidance and proper Christian instruction, lest they stray too far from the Constitution and the flag. It was the white-based culture that had come to be recognised throughout the world as so very American, they affirmed, apple pie and the fourth of July – ignoring the fact that the country's black and Hispanic citizens, along with the melting-pot collection of ethnicities from all parts of the world, had a right to share in this culture and were, indeed, very much a major part of it, too. Only a white commentator would stumble over this obvious disconnect. Ali saw it, though; he saw it as clear as day.

He had one more fight after Terrell and, after a tough opening, turned it into another master class. When he defended his title against the number-one contender, Zora Folley, in front of 13,780 fans at Madison Square Garden, the gate takings of $244,471 broke a record for the venue at the time. Ali was unquestionably on the rise, albeit with the snipers still taking aim from the shrubbery. But this night, as a 7–1 on favourite, he was just about at the height of his powers. The fans were not to know this would be his last appearance in a ring for three and a half years, and he left them with a special finish to remember. He had toyed with the excellent Folley for half a dozen rounds and, after urgings from his new manager, Herbert Muhammad, he knocked his bedazzled opponent out without ceremony and with much ease: a pair of rights leaving Folley in a heap, face down on the famous canvas.

In this sort of fight Ali was hugely comfortable. He was more at home in a boxing ring than nearly any other fighter of his generation. It was his personal stage, the place from where he made his statements to the world, showing them time and again that he actually was The Greatest. Folley was the ninth challenger of his title. But Ali had a different confrontation to deal with now, with no gloves, no chance for a knockout, and the other side would bring the referee.

Ali says the letter demanding he appear for induction into the armed forces, at 'Local Board No 61 ... [at] 3rd Floor, 701 San Jacinto St, Houston, Texas, 77022 on April 28 1967 at 8.30 a.m.' arrived at his home on April Fool's Day. He always saw these sorts of hilarious details in even the heaviest moment. And this would be serious stuff he had to deal with. The time for word play and poems had passed. This was a real fight. And he discovered that everyone knew about it. Walking in downtown Chicago, he heard people shouting, 'They gotcha! They gotcha! Sonofabitch! Thank God they gotcha!' They held up headlines in the local paper. The news had been cleverly leaked. This was an orchestrated campaign and Uncle Sam had landed the first punch.

It has to be said, he'd done himself no favours in his attitude towards Terrell. Even Milton Gross in the *New York Post*, a writer Ali considered an ally, was moved to write about his taunting of his opponent, 'Boxing is a brutal business but always, before Clay brought a sadistic streak to it, there was a community between fighters.' There was – Gross was right. Ali, although he struggled to see it, was wrong. If the dirty business of professional fighting were to have any integrity it surely resided in the way boxers conducted themselves in the ring. Dignity is tough to hang on to if you are being personally humiliated in front of thousands of people. And fighters, with some notable exceptions, did have that unspoken awareness. They could beat a guy up, but leave a little of him to get him through the night. Ali now was totally destroying his opponents, physically and mentally. It seemed he had lost sight of that precept of respect. He was angry, very angry. And that anger was burning a hole in him. It would take him a long time to come to terms with that. What sustained him was his very deep sense of defiance. It has stayed with him all his life, not always to his benefit, but he was true to himself, for better or worse.

He refused military induction, as he said he would, and it was explained to him that he had now set sail on a route that would lead to imprisonment, if convicted. He was not remotely concerned. He had utter belief in his own righteousness and that of his religious advisers. They were a tight unit, drawing strength from each other and transferring it to their most famous disciple, the man now much more famous than the Nation's leader, Elijah Muhammad – who would come to resent Ali's celebrity. But, in the first exchanges, they could not beat the system. On 20 June, an all-white jury convicted Ali and he was sentenced to five years in prison. He immediately appealed and the process dragged on with glacial turgidity. In all – because the boxing authorities fell into line with the courts and refused to allow him to work as a fighter – Ali was out of the ring between March 1967 and October 1970. The ban and the conviction, as well as the appeal process, robbed him of his best years, between the ages of twenty-five and twenty-nine. It was a travesty.

But Ali bore the burden with calm resignation, housing his anger in a series of nationwide lectures in universities who were home now to a growing number of students disenchanted and disgusted with the progress of the war in Vietnam. He had, almost accidentally, inherited an audience in tune with his protest. They got to know a different Ali, an articulate, funny yet serious polemicist, who could argue his case in his own fashion, devoid of pretension, stripped down to its basics and zeroing in on the principles of freedom of expression, one of the core tenets of the American Constitution. Intentionally or not, Ali was rebuilding his reputation with rhetoric that now struck a chord beyond his own black constituency. These students cared little for the objectives of the Nation of Islam but they were concerned with inalienable rights. They did care that a man should be able to stand up, without fear of arrest or hindrance, and tell the world what he believed. The fact that young American soldiers were dying in fields in faraway Vietnam only strengthened his position. Maybe he was right about that, too. Perhaps America had no business fighting in those God-forsaken cities and towns in a country that few cared for or knew that much about. It had started as an ideological war, a war against Communism, the dreaded devil that was always gnawing at the gate. But the Communists were winning. Or at least they were not losing, like they were supposed to. They had not succumbed. They had disappeared into their tunnels, emerging to blow the legs off young Americans who now were reduced to cartoon characters, wandering through jungle battlefields stoned and listening to The Doors. It seemed like the whole of the American entertainment industry would eventually descend on Vietnam, sifting through the bones for significance and meaning. And they would find Ali still standing, 'still a nigger'.

Chapter Nine
Jungle Beat

Vietnam had begun to recede from the popular consciousness in America as the 1970s rolled on. It was a reviled war, an embarrassment. Servicemen returning from the term of duty would land in San Diego and disappear into the hinterland there rather than go home, finding refuge in drugs or alcohol. There were not many homecomings, in fact. Not many yellow ribbons around the old oak tree, the symbol of thanksgiving for sacrifice, in victory or defeat. But this was the war America no longer wanted, and the young men who died for its cause were, in many cases, abandoned as collateral damage. It was a very sad time for a proud country.

But there was Ali again. Still there; still punching; still talking. He got his licence back, dismissed Jerry Quarry in three one-sided rounds in Atlanta – the only place that would take the fight – in October

1970. Across the United States and Canada, 206 outlets took the fight on closed-circuit TV. They showed it just about everywhere else too. There was a considerable hunger to see Ali, who'd reconstructed his reputation with the help of the university students who were prepared to listen to his message while he was in exile. His media friends returned to the fold, aggrieved on his behalf, especially as the legal process seemed to be dragging out until the end of time. Howard Cosell was among his most ardent advocates. For all their kidding, he turned out to be a true friend. And Ali looked pretty good for someone who'd been away for three and a half years.

He soon enough had his conviction lifted. Ali was legit again – and that suited everyone: the boxing public, the TV stations, the promoters and the rest of the heavyweight division. The sport had been fairly dull in his absence and he was about to resume as noisily as anyone would expect. He would be slower, of course, throwing more punches from a flat-footed stance, with less dancing, but with all the instincts still in place. Superman just decided to return to earth.

And there, in one of the most bizarre settings for any fight, he made such an impact that he earned the right to be regarded once again as King of the World. That is an interesting title for David Remnick's book on Ali, first published in 1998 and sub-titled, *Muhammad Ali and the Rise of an American Hero*. But Remnick leaves the story in the 1960s. Ali's second coronation was completed in the jungle, in the home of his ancestors, a return to his ancient roots. It was a weird and magical occasion, stretched over a couple of months, accompanied by a concert, filmed brilliantly and shrouded in all the magic of a great Ali occasion. That is why he was so great. He brought something special to every occasion, from walking into a room to knocking out the awesome George Foreman in the eighth round of their fight in front of the quite despicable despot, Zaire's Mobutu Sese Seko Kuku Ngbendu wa Za Banga, who ruled from 1965 until 1997. It could be said Ali played his part in extending that cruel governance of one of the poorest countries in the world. None of that concerned either Ali or Foreman – or the man who put the fight together, Don King. They were, remember, part of the fight game. A lot of bad things happened in the fight game. They were just there for the fighting, not for the rest of it. Did that argument stand up? Not really. We are all master of our own actions. Ali gave up three and a half years of his career in defence of that principle. He risked prison by standing up for his religious beliefs. And he took $5 million to fight in Mobutu's Rumble in the

Jungle, because it was Mobutu's Rumble, really, not Ali's. It was Ali who made it happen and he took the money upfront that King scared up in London, through Barclays Bank, and the intervention of John Daly, a member of a well-known south London boxing family who would go on to be a Hollywood producer. Daly was the intermediary who pulled many of the interested parties together – and, as a prize, he got to commentate on the fight for the film version, *When We Were Kings*.

It was not a savoury episode. It had little to recommend it morally. But, that said, the fight lives in the memory as one of the truly great boxing events. In every way, from the setting to the result, it dripped in drama. The final right hand with which Ali floors Foreman, which won him back the title at thirty-two, was near perfect. The right hand that had decked Liston in their 1965 rematch, despite all suspicions, was probably of a similar force, except it was not so visible. There was no missing this blow. When George wheeled and collapsed, his dazed head rising briefly from the canvas to see nothing much but the jungle night, the deed was done. It was a minor miracle. Not a single respected voice spoke up for Ali beforehand. Not one. He was 40–1 with some bookmakers and most experts feared for his safety. But he worked his magic and his reputation soared again.

The Cassius Clay I adored when shadow-boxing as a ten-year-old was back. He'd just changed his name – and his shape. He didn't move like an angel anymore, but he still delivered miracles. Like he always said he would. How could we ever have doubted him? This was the real genius of Muhammad Ali: he made you believe. He was like some sort of huckster who turned out to be real. And the more he kept proving doubters wrong, the stronger was the conviction among believers that there would be no end to his heroics. For as long as he wanted to, he would keep winning. It was all an illusion, of course. We were all fools – including Ali. He would be acquainted with his folly, though, not in defeat but in victory.

Remarkably, what was to follow in the final great win of his career was gruesome. And, even as he neared the exit, there were other signs of degradation. He was philandering on a wild and uncaring scale now, seemingly oblivious to the hurt he might be causing to those close to him. He did not appear to care. It was as if he thought he was above normal judgment. The man with so much love in him was giving too much of it away to the wrong people, and it all unravelled in a pretty ugly sequence, nowhere more publicly than in Manila the following year.

The last round of the Vietnam fight will be forever remembered in that stark image of retreat by over-loaded helicopters from the roof of the American Embassy on 29 April 1975, with locals begging for passage, knowing the fate that awaited them as the Viet Cong crowded through the streets of the capital, looking for retribution. There was no righteousness left in the struggle now. Ali had moved through the next chapter of his story and was thirteen fights from its conclusion.

Chapter Ten
A Fight Too Far

Not content with doing business with one right-wing autocrat, Ali moved on to the Philippines, where Ferdinand Marcos and his outlandish wife, Imelda, ruled over another poor and under-resourced people. The international euphemism for a dictator is 'strongman' – interpret that as you like, but Marcos brooked no interference with his reign. He might not have been as ruthless as Mobutu, but he was tough enough. Corruption and nepotism marked his rule, and he spent his fading years in exile in Hawaii.

But, when Ali rumbled on from the jungle to the Araneta Coliseum in Quezon City in October 1975, he brought more than just an entourage and an attitude. He brought his mistress and a dark heart. It was, paradoxically, his most astounding performance in the ring, but not one of his finest moments as a human being.

This was going to be the crowning of his trilogy with Joe Frazier. You might imagine that after two fights, with a win apiece – the first, Frazier's, a classic – there would be a sufficient well of mutual respect to guard against descent into trash talking and insult. No chance. Ali was out of control. Indeed, he had been for some time. He had developed a sense of entitlement, driven by his considerable ego, that led him to believe he could say and do what he wanted without consequence. Of course, he defended every excess as an expression of his near-boundless personality, and said he was only selling tickets and gaining a psychological edge over his opponent. All true. But all of it: not just the bits that suited Ali. He was as bad as he was entertaining. He was as uncaring for others as he was committed to putting on a show. There was no excuse for it – except that it all existed within the circus tent of professional boxing, an environment that had not changed since those Georgian nobles had sponsored the barbarism that passed for sponsored fighting two centuries and more ago.

That was the tradition Ali was living up to. He was not the member of a ballet corps; he did not belong to an orchestra or a poetry society. He was a boxer, a fighter, and he carried a fighter's mentality with him twenty-four hours a day. He was used to conflict; he welcomed it. Conflict is what he lived for. So an argument with his wife the day before the fight over the presence of his mistress in the same hotel was of a piece with going out to tear into Joe Frazier. As gentle and caring as he could be, Ali survived on his ability to bring animosity to nearly everything he did when he needed to. If he ever lost that ability, he would be dead in the ring – perhaps literally. It was that dangerous a place – and rarely more so than on that October morning – scheduled to hit TV peak times in the United States.

The fight itself was as brutal as anyone present could recall. Those of us who have watched only footage of it get a filtered view, of course, but it is still frightening to watch. It did not seem right to pay to watch two men go this close to extinction. You wanted to reach inside the screen, go back in time and put a hand between them, beg them to desist, to stop hating each other and to go home. But that, again, is to misunderstand the exercise. There can be no limits, except those imposed by rule makers. And at no time did either the noble Frazier or Ali break any rules. They fought a clean, murderous battle.

Ali took the early stages, Frazier the middle section, and Ali was finishing with more precision and discipline against Frazier's half-blind courage as they neared the conclusion. The fourteenth round was cruel in the extreme. Ali battered Frazier, his one good eye now closing fast, rendering him a walking – or rather stumbling – target for three minutes. When they returned to their stools, Ali had hit the wall. Despite what Ali's trainer Angelo Dundee would insist vehemently ever after, there is a strong suggestion that the fighter wanted to quit. In the other corner, Frazier's trainer, Eddie Futch, made it easier for his man. He refused to let him come out for even one more round, even though there was little in the fight and a concluding assault might well have won it for him. Futch, in my opinion, proved himself by some way to be the better trainer and better human being than Dundee that day. He put boxing in context. It was no longer a sporting occasion, nor even a business proposition. This was getting down to life and death – and Futch voted for life.

As it happens, neither man would be the same after this horrific experience. And both boxed on for another six years – although they never met again in the ring. Thank God for that small mercy.

Chapter Eleven
King on Ali

In the summer of 2014, I spent a few days with Don King in Cairo. He was there trying to persuade the government to bankroll a world heavyweight title fight between his WBC champion, Bermane Stiverne, a thirty-five-year-old Haitian whose ten years in Las Vegas were remarkable only for the fact he did not own a television, and the mandatory challenger, Deontay Wilder, whose record since turning professional after winning bronze for the United States at the Beijing Olympics sent a chill through the business: thirty-one fights, thirty-one knockouts.

Stiverne was King's wild card return from obscurity. He had been marginalised since Mike Tyson's final fall, although he did promote a world-class fighter in Tavoris Cloud. However, after Cloud lost to the ageless Bernard Hopkins in 2013, King was considered just another player in a game he used to rule. Hopkins once was a King fighter – how the wheel whirls. Now Stiverne, a peripheral player in the heavyweight division until he announced his arrival by knocking out Chris Arreola in May 2014, to win the WBC version of the heavyweight title vacated by Vitali Klitschko, was going to haul King back to where he felt most comfortable – the limelight.

I went to Cairo to cover the story of his comeback for the newspapers I write for, the *Guardian* and the *Observer*, and to discuss with King the possibility of making a documentary about his very interesting life. He was open to that, although I knew from many years of watching him operate that negotiations would not be straightforward. A collaborator on the project, the British film director Paul Martin, had sent King a copy of *Senna* on behalf of his business partner, James Gay-Rees, who produced that award-winning film. It seemed to do the trick: he liked the film and reckoned Paul and James might be the people who could best tell his story. However, at that moment they were finishing off another film, on the life of Cristiano Ronaldo, and were in Japan with the footballer just as King was arriving in Egypt. I wondered if he would regard their absence as a snub, but it did not seem to bother him. He had his hands full with the fight project. For now, his head was full of Pharaohs and Sphinxes, as he worked one room after another, impressing his hosts in the Egyptian Ministry of Tourism with his energy and unique presentational skills.

We had a bit of history, King and I, as I had spent a couple of days with him in New York City in 2001, for a piece in the now-defunct *Observer Sports Monthly*. I knew he was a master of connection and got to witness the skill first hand. On the first day of that trip, I watched him in court, a place with which he was very familiar. The details of the case are not important but what happened subsequently was far more interesting. That night, the photographer Andy Hall and I met King in an Italian restaurant, Bravo Gianni on the Upper East Side, along with Emanuel Steward, who was training Lennox Lewis at the time. Lewis was one of the participants in the complicated legal proceedings in Court 14A of the Southern District Court of New York, down in Pearl Street. He did not accompany us to dinner, perhaps because he was suing Hasim Rahman, who had knocked him out three weeks earlier in South Africa to take his world heavyweight title – and King and Rahman were in litigation. Or maybe he didn't want to shell out $25 for the osso buco veal knuckle. He missed a treat.

Over dinner, King revealed that this was the restaurant in which he had given Rahman $500,000 in cash, a sum of money that ensured his signature on a fight contract. Steward, who wanted Lewis to fight Rahman as soon as possible in a rematch, smiled knowingly, raising an eyebrow. This was also the place King used to come in the old days with Ali, whose face stares down from the wall alongside the eponymous owner, Gianni, who at that point was still running the place and, attached to old-fashioned cooking values, insisted all the staff wear tuxedos. Bravo Gianni is now closed; King is still going. There was a slew of anecdotes that night – all of them King's. Steward calls him 'an instrument of God'. We agreed to continue the conversation the following day.

It is not often a white reporter gets through the literal and figurative barriers that guard the Nation of Islam, who of course were once maligned as the Black Muslims, but King opened that door for Andy and myself in the summer of 2001. As he guided us past the security checks in the foyer, James Brown's sister, Fanny, spotted King and implored him to get her in. He said he'd do his best. So, there we were, half an hour or so later, talking to Louis Farrakhan, the current leader of the religious group. The Nation were in town for a conference, and the soldiers – for that is how they regard themselves – eyed us with suspicion as we came and then went after our audience with Farrakhan, the Bronx-born son of West Indian parents who once was called Louis Wolcott, attracted interest as a young violin prodigy and sang calypso songs for a living under the show-business name of The Charmer. The conversation with Farrakhan was stilted and he called King 'incomparable'. He is not wrong.

After that weird interlude, King said he had one more surprise for us. As we walked across town from the Nation's convention, people waved and called out to him every few yards, and he loved it. 'Only in America!' he responded. 'Yessiree, Only in America! Heh, heh!' By the time we got to the Rihga Royal Hotel, the destination of our final treat, he had agreed to my dare to try to stop New York traffic in rush hour. He approached a traffic cop, and the deal was done. Andy took the photo – while lying on his belly on an intersection of 7th Avenue – to provide the proof, and that made a memorable cover of the following edition of the *Observer Sports Monthly*.

So, why did we go to the Rihga? When King opened the door to a penthouse suite that might have cost $1,000 a night or more, there stood Muhammad Ali. This was networking of the highest order. Andy, who has photographed plenty of celebrities, was as word shy as the man he found himself staring at. For a couple of hours, which passed far too quickly for both of us, we listened and watched King and Ali trade stories and laughs. We laughed too, but contributed little else to the entertainment. King's phone rang – it was the actor Will Smith, who was filming a movie about Ali in New York that night, down at 23rd and 10th Avenue, near Madison Square Garden. King handed the phone to the real Ali. 'Hey, that's me on the phone!' Ali jokes, after hearing Smith's near-perfect impression of him.

I found it difficult to watch them interact without casting a thought back to their association when Ali was boxing – and was so loud. Now he barely spoke above a whisper. But there was a light in his eyes, still, and he made you feel good just by sharing the same oxygen. He did his magic tricks, as he invariably does for guests, he told some dreadful jokes and he generally had a ball. He loved being with King, he really did. They bounced gags off each other like a couple of teenagers and their banter was something of a comedy routine.

This is some of the dialogue I taped that night for the magazine article:

'Every knee must bend,' King started up, 'every head must bow, every tongue must confess: thou art The Greatest, The Greatest of a-a-a-a-ll times! Muhammad. Muhammad Ali. That's my man. The history.'

'Yeah, but I a bum.'

'You ain't never be a bum, man. I want to take you to China with me [this was a reference to an upcoming promotion King had planned to introduce boxing to that country].'

[Ali then starts in with his jokes ...]

'A black man, a Mexican, a Puerto Rican riding in the back of a car. Who's drivin? The police.'

'What did Abe Lincoln say when he woke up from a two-day drunk? I freed who?'

'What's the difference between a Jew and a canoe? A canoe tips.'

That sounded weird. It probably did to King's public relations man, Richard Rubenstein, although he showed no discomfort.

There was a revealing exchange when Leonard Muhammad, one of the Nation heavy hitters who had come with us from the convention, said King was giving up pork to comply with the tenets of Islam. Ali made a noise like a pig. More tear-streaming laughter filled the room. No way was King giving up pork. He loves his food – and has no known sympathy for pigs.

But he paid lip service to his respect for the Nation, not altogether convincingly.

'I understood, I recognised my sins, brother! But God didn't come to save the righteous. He came to save the sinners. All of you who have been so righteous, pious and holier than I am, I mean you're there, but, for us sinners, I submit, humbly, to the fire and the mercy of the Lord! All praise to the Lord!'

Ali, theatrically, interjected: 'You shall burn in hell!'

'In the fieriest fires of hell! Heh, heh, heh, heh! All right! He's God's child.'

What I was not fully aware of as this sideshow unfolded was how much Ali resented the hold the Nation had on him. He gave up his membership of the sect when Farrakhan became leader, although he is still a practising Muslim.

Andy wanted his photo taken with Ali, so King took the camera.

'Andy, I shall be your photographer! The little button right there? Aw, yes! That's it, yes. It's focus, focus, focus and then you hit the little button right there. Open your eyes, champ! Open your eyes. Heeeehaaah! Hey team! Muhammad, don't you give me no jive, You gonna go out in five!'

Ali, Lonnie's wife and nurse, scolded King when he went over the top.

'You gotta get in shape, champ. This guy started me off, you know, fresh outta the penitentiary.'

Lonnie: 'Oh, great, Don. Thanks. Great copy.'

But it was. It was all great copy. The story wrote itself. I just turned on the tape recorder and transcribed one hilarious exchange after another. A monkey could have done it, as they say. Both of them are born salesmen, they know how to sell themselves and their product – except the merchandise has changed for Ali. He's not selling fights any more. He's selling peace and understanding. King? He'd be selling carpets on the corner, if he had to, but he's happy to do peace and understanding. Many years after this wild night, he would get a chance to prove it ...

King had never been to Egypt, but Ali had – in June 1964, three months after he won the title from Sonny Liston in Miami. However, Ali did not come to Africa to sell a fight: he came to sell religion. He'd revealed to the world after beating Liston that he had been a member of the Nation of Islam since he was eighteen and, now that he was world champion, he was changing his name from Cassius Clay to Muhammad Ali. If he'd burnt the Stars and Stripes on the steps of the Washington Monument while singing 'The Internationale' he could not have been more unpopular in his own country.

Ali's faith would drive him from that point onwards. It would put him at odds with his government, rob him of his peak boxing years, as well as the potential to earn many millions of dollars, and, ultimately, come to define him every bit as much as his sport did. He turned a name that was unfamiliar to white audiences into a passport to more lasting acclaim: Ali – Just three letters; easy to remember, impossible to forget. He put what he called his slave name, Cassius Clay, into the past. It took a while, but he was accepted in the end.

And there I was, on a wretchedly hot night, in a coffee shop in an ancient bazaar in Cairo, with dawn approaching, and King was reminiscing about the most exciting times of his life: his days with a man he loved but betrayed – only to be forgiven then reconciled, the ultimate journey of redemption. What, I wondered, did he really make of Ali?

'I started at the top,' he grinned. 'I started with Muhammad Ali!' he laughed. King finds humour in conversation so often because he is never far from irony, or irreverence for society's norms. He laughs at life and his critics in equal measure. Laughter is his shield. And he guards his past. But he can never escape the long-range glow of Ali. The fighter made the promoter, no question. King knows it, too.

'I see him maybe six months ago. The only thing is his loquaciousness, his verbalisation is impaired, you know?' Only King could call the ability to talk a lot 'loquaciousness' or 'verbalisation', lending something normal a higher status. It is a method, a technique. It is wreathed in sarcasm, almost a slap in the face of high-mindedness, a punch to the kidneys of his one-time masters. Chris Eubank, who walked tall in British boxing for a while, employed the same ruse, dressing in jodhpurs and sporting a monocle he did not need, embroidering his every utterance in absurd, mock poshness that he would abandon the moment he met up with those who knew him best.

'But he's still sharp,' King continued, 'his mind is still going. He's a tremendous guy. You know, nobody can tell how great he really was. At the height of his career, he was four years in exile for standing up for what he believes in. Then, miraculously, after being in exile, after the United

States exonerated him … well, you can't tell what this boy could have been. He's just a phenomenal, God-blessed individual. All the blessings of Allah were poured upon him.'

We were, after all, in Egypt – and King was pushing a fight. So there were bound to be plenty of references to Islam and Allah and our wonderful guests. He has not lost the power to persuade.

After a pause, he continued: 'What a man. He's fantastic. He gave up the trivial values, the money and whatever, to stand up for what he believed in, a conscientious objector, disciple of Elijah Muhammad. It cost him a lot of money but it gained him mortality. He was religious and they raked him over the coals.'

I get what he means. Language is no more than a basis for negotiation for King, sometimes, in the art of communication. And I got the strong impression King would like a slice of that immortality. He has the notoriety, fame and money, but he hasn't got what Ali got for himself: universal love. King knows that, he's no fool. He knows people struggle to accept him because of his own murky past: two killings, lots of litigation, relationships forged then thrown away. But I believe him when he says he loves and respects Ali, whatever the sins he committed against him.

There is an axis in this relationship that is revealing. Ali needs to do nothing but be alive to engender love and admiration. He sits at home, mostly, and takes the occasional phone call, replies to the still-steady stream of letters and messages, and he smiles quietly. His face now is not animated, but it is content. His eyes tell all the stories he has been part of. It is a knowing look, still. It speaks to a past that is more famous and celebrated than that of anyone he has shared time with in his lifetime. If he died tomorrow, he would die a happy, if imperfect, man.

And King? Well, he is a different character altogether. He too has a past, good and bad. But he wrestles with it still. He is not content and is, in fact, lonely. He spends long hours at his home in Florida alone. He does not speak much to his family, his sons and a daughter. His wife died a few years ago, and his friends are mostly on the end of a telephone. George Bush Snr rings him occasionally to chat. He has other friends from the past who still call, but he is not as famous as he was – and that is a spear in his side. King craved fame – as did Ali, of course. It gave them credibility that white society otherwise would deny them. They did not want acclaim for the sake of it; they wanted it to make a statement about who they were. They shared that with all black Americans. But fame and all its trappings come at a price.

Ali handled that burden in his own way. He stood up to the people who were trying to tell him who he should be – and even what his name should be. He would not be told. Just like Jack Johnson. And unlike Joe Louis, who succumbed to the pressure of the Establishment and who, towards the end of his life, regretted doing so. Ali, however, had an inner strength that allowed him to rise above the crowd. He did not always use it properly, and he did not see in the quiet dignity of Joe Frazier, for instance, that others were fighting the fight in their own way. Ali chose confrontation – or, at least, he agreed with the confrontation that the Nation of Islam chose for him: rejection of the draft for service in Vietnam.

'It gave him the kind of strength that was different,' King says. 'Before, he was the stereotype image of the black. He was lazy, lethargic, we can't write or read, all lie, cheat and steal, we're sinners and savages, we're shiftless, worthless, no account.'

That is an image of black Americans King has of himself and has repeated, like a mantra, for as long as I can remember. He used those same words during our time together in New York in 2001. He has been fighting against the perception all his life, not always successfully. 'Perception becomes reality,' he says. And he lumps Ali into that bin, too. While it is hard to remember that characterisation of Cassius Clay as some cartoon stereotype from an old movie, I think I know where King is coming from. He is speaking in the most general terms, and he is probably on the money. Prejudice is born of image.

He goes off on a slight but relevant tangent. King knew the mother of Colin Powell, the American general who made a name for himself during the first Iraq War, and was even courted by the Republicans as a possible presidential candidate. King claims Powell's mother played the numbers on his patch – won it, and sent young Colin to university on the proceeds. It is some story; it might even be true. Now, he looks back on that association and sees another strand to the black narrative, and not one that enthuses him.

'He thought he could maybe assimilate. But the time was coming when he was called to meet the press, and they started painting him in those stereotypes too. It came back to what it is, you know what I mean?'

The day before I left Cairo, I was sitting in our hotel, having lunch with King and a few others – including people from the Tourism ministry, who had been at our side throughout the trip. They were not eating; it was Ramadan. King and I were tucking in, he a little more enthusiastically than myself, I have to add. He ordered the soup of the day, Caesar salad, spaghetti Bolognese, rack of lamb and lots of water. Our hosts did not blink. King didn't finish all of his food, but he looked sated.

There was a lull in the chat and I asked him if Ali still fasted during Ramadan. 'Uh, yeah,' he said. 'I think he does.' I do not doubt that Ali adheres to his religion's demands, but this is the right answer, given the circumstances. It suits the situation. King knows what to say and when.

He said he found Ali in good spirits when they last met, although subdued by the Parkinson's disease that had gripped him since 1984, twenty years after he beat Liston, ten years after he beat Foreman in Zaire, three years after he lost to Trevor Berbick. Ali has been a man of the ages almost since the day he was born.

'Man, he is so special,' King said, tracking back to our conversation the night before, as he tended to do, as if all his thoughts were on a programmed loop. It is difficult often to divine the real from the surreal with King (even that sounds like something he would come out with). It is as if you are playing a never-ending word game with him – but for what reason? He determines the agenda every time, just as he did with Ali and a host of other fighters, including Tyson. Many of them regretted the experience. But Ali forgave King – that is the remarkable fact about their relationship.

King's part in the closing chapter of Ali's boxing career was a sorry one. Three months before he fought Larry Holmes in Las Vegas in 1980, the Nevada State Athletic Commission – one of the few in America with even a shred of credibility – stipulated that Ali should submit himself to neurological tests at the Mayo Clinic, one of the most respected hospitals in the world, to assess if he were suffering from brain damage that might embarrass all of them. He was, of course, only a shell of the great fighter he once had been. But this was insurance, not compassion.

Shamefully, the boxing authorities went through the motions of doing the right thing but did not release the results of those tests. What they showed when eventually made public was this: Ali could not touch his finger to his nose, his speech was scrambled, he could not easily jump on one foot, something that had been second nature to him during the peak of his career, an exercise to encourage balance and coordination. Suitably comforted, however, Nevada thought it was fine to let Ali expose his failing health to the attentions of a vibrant and dangerous champion in Holmes. All parties – fighters, promoters, and the alleged governing body – were satisfied. Boxing is a business built on compromise and amnesia.

What happened in that fight was the sad unravelling of a legend. Harry Mullan, editor of *Boxing News*, was at that fight. Few people knew more about boxing than Mullan, who became a good friend. 'I don't like to tell people this,' he said not long before he died, 'but I cried at that fight. It was the most shameful thing I had ever seen, a great fighter – probably the greatest – posturing in the ring, pretending to be part of a competitive sporting occasion, and his friend and former sparring partner reluctantly beating him up. All of it was for money. None of it was for the integrity of the sport. I was ashamed to be part of it.'

Ali got $8 million. Holmes, the champion, making the eighth defence of his title, received $2.3 million. I do not know what King made from the fight. It will have been substantial.

'Ah, yes,' King concluded, 'what a great fighter, great man. I love him dearly still.'

And I suddenly remembered how that night ended, thirteen years before in a New York hotel. As we walked towards the door, King put his arm around Ali and they whispered something. King planted a delicate kiss on Ali's cheek. Ali looked to be chuckling to himself, and says, 'Yeah ... and still a nigger!'

Chapter Twelve
Silence

Muhammad Ali was diagnosed with Parkinson's disease in 1984, three years after he stopped boxing. But the signs of decline had been there for years, certainly for much of his comeback. His speech was slurred, his movement sluggish, his smile a little less convincing. His wit did not slow, but the delivery did. He was still capable of the sharpest observation, the funniest little remark. He reverted, somewhat, to the innocent child he had once been. He embraced children, especially, reinforcing his love for them at every opportunity, and they responded.

He left many in his wake, either fellow fighters or those wise guys in the media. Cosell is long gone. Frazier, too. Larry Holmes, his good friend and one-time sparring partner who went on to be a very fine champion, is still with us and in decent shape. Ken Norton, who broke his jaw, is dead. Norman Mailer is dead. Don King is not dead – well, not the last time I looked.

Ali's survival is not a badge he wears, it is just his lot in life. He rarely leaves his home now and rumours surface regularly of his failing health. At the time of writing, he was still with us. It will be very hard for many of us to come to terms with his death when it arrives. He will leave the most enormous void.

But what we will always have is his legacy – and that is considerable. What he has created cannot be torn down. For all his waywardness at various points of his interesting life, he will leave in credit – massively so. He has spread such love and affection, and opened so many eyes to various injustices, that we have to forgive him his sins – as if it is in our gift to do so in the first place. Certainly he would do so in reverse. He has forgiven just about everyone who has sinned against him, lied to him, robbed him. Joe Frazier forgave him, and that very much was the measure of the man. Ali was needlessly cruel to Frazier, but that is done. There is no going back.

What matters is that we see his achievements in a bigger context, his contribution to his race: the human race. We cannot walk in his shoes but we have witnessed him on that road to freedom. He picked up from Jack Johnson in some respects, irreverent at every turn, but also from wider readings, from observations of life.

Like Joe Louis, whom he did not really resemble in many ways as a human being, he brought respect for black people with the wondrousness of his glove work. He was, quite simply, magnificent. It doesn't matter if he was better than Louis – or Dempsey or Marciano or any of the other heavyweights mentioned in the same breath; he was great in his own right and on many, many nights. He inspired so many fighters that followed. Ask boxers of a certain generation – say, anyone born in the 1960s – and they will invariably mention Ali as their favourite fighter, the one boxer who provided them with the belief and strength to give it a go. He didn't quite give me enough of that inspiration, but no great loss there.

Today, Floyd Mayweather Jnr is The Greatest. Not for all times, as Ali used to say, but of his generation, probably. And he inherits a lot of what has gone before, some of the style and presentation of Ali, the sport's original showman, the one fighter who brought the sport to life for the entire planet. Nobody really had done it quite so completely. Mayweather is big – certainly the richest, most successful and most influential figure in professional boxing today – but he is not Muhammad Ali.

Nor was Mike Tyson, who adores Ali still. Tyson, in fact, goes to blubbering jelly in his presence, unable to hide his love for the man. And what is incontrovertible is that since Trevor Berbick beat Ali in 1981, to close the book on his career, there has been nobody else to take his place. Most likely, there never will be. That is both a disturbing and comforting thought. It fills hearts with regret but describes the achievements of the man: he is irreplaceable.

People of all ages, races and background had a take on Ali. Overwhelmingly, it is positive.

Author and poet Maya Angelou, who died in 2014, said of him: 'I think that a great deal of the respect and affection that people of every colour have for Muhammad Ali can be laid at the door of his manliness. That doesn't mean bravado or strength. That means that he is a great man.'

Mickey Duff, promoter, who also died in 2014, said: 'First and foremost, he was an even greater human being than he was a fighter ...'

There is no underestimating the narcissism of boxers – or what appears to be so. They are essentially shy and insecure athletes who must constantly reassure themselves of their worth, because they can trust only themselves. Mayweather's take on Floyd Mayweather, for instance, is a loud if typical expression of this emotion: 'I don't care what people say about Floyd Mayweather. I live for me. Love me or hate me, you're gonna watch me.' It could be Ali talking. Mayweather, whether he knows it or not, got that from Ali, maybe even from Jack Johnson.

'I don't have to be what you want me to be,' Ali said when asked why he was not part of the civil rights movement. And, when a reporter called him Cassius, he was similarly steadfast about who he really was: 'I'm not your slave. I'm Muhammad Ali.'

So, in 2014, fifty years after he won the world heavyweight title from Sonny Liston, Ali is as strong in our consciousness as he ever was. That is some achievement for an ailing man of seventy-two who spends most of his days waiting for someone to bring him his tablets.

I remember Ali in many guises and situations. I can see him now, his shaking arm as he lit the flame at the Atlanta Olympics in 1996. There was a universal sucking in of breath around the planet as the breeze picked up and flames licked his sleeve. I turned to a couple of colleagues in the press seats on the other side of the stadium and I knew we were thinking the same thing: could he do it? Of course he could. He'd never really let me down, except the handful of times when he foolishly fought when he should not have done. Did he have to do this? I think he did. He never ducked a challenge in his life. However, as he steadied his trembling right arm – the one that rattled the chins of Sonny Liston, George Foreman and Joe Frazier – I had a split-second of doubt. I reached out to him, as did millions of others I'm sure, and willed him to get the job done, this ritual that was both trivial and significant at the same time, a gesture that mattered in the context of the Olympics, the illuminating of a long-cherished myth. He touched the final connection to the cauldron above (which comically resembled a chip holder from McDonald's), and the deed was complete. A final knockout victory for a champion of the world.

Yet, for all that the image of Ali lighting that flame will never die, my recollections go further back, to the time when he was full of life, every muscle and bone moving in uncanny syncopation with his quicksilver brain. In the practice of his art, Ali never looked ungainly. Not once in sixty-one paid contests. Even when Joe Frazier put him down, he fell with a sort of choreographed grace. When his head hit the bottom rope after Henry Cooper had uncorked his famous left hook on to the most overworked jaw in sport, he lolled, eyes glazed, as if he meant to be there, resting. He was so wonderfully coordinated a mover, so smooth and powerful, yet light-footed and balletic, that everything around him moved to his rhythm. Sugar Ray Robinson once said that the secret to boxing was to dictate the pace and space of a fight, to force an opponent to fit in between your own movements, to make him move without even touching him. Ali did that. Except when under the most extreme pressure (usually from Frazier), he used the ring as if it were a park in which to take a stroll, throwing out punches as he went. Few missed.

That was the bedrock of Ali's appeal. His special gift was the very narrowly defined skill of boxing. It made him what he was, and we often sat speechless in admiration. Boxing gave him not only a platform from which to launch a thousand tirades but it provided the perfect stage for his demonstrations, which is what many of his fights were. He embodied the other quality needed to box: courage. Few fighters had a better chin. Very few were as willing to get up once down. He lit a fire under the world in the twenty-one years he fought as a professional, and the embers are still glowing. Ali the boxer was also Ali the human being, loud in the beginning, humbled at the finish. His journey was glorious, joyous, painful and sad. It was, in short, life. Fighting is that elemental and raw. When conducted as art, it reaches another level, but it is fundamentally not far removed from the struggle for survival human beings have always realised was their lot.

So, what is it we learnt from Muhammad Ali, then? Maybe just one thing: humanity.

A Short Reading List

Ali, Muhammad, and Durham, Richard *The Greatest: My Own Story*, Random House, 1975.

Collings, Mark *Muhammad Ali: Through the Eyes of the World*, MPG Books, 2001.

Early, Gerald *I'm a Little Special, a Muhammad Ali Reader*, Yellow Jersey Press, 1998.

Miller, Davis *The Tao of Muhammad Ali*, Vintage, 1997.

Newfield, Jack *Only in America: The Life and Crimes of Don King*, Williams Morrow, 1995.

Remnick, David *King of the World: Muhammad Ali and the Rise of an American Hero*, Random House, 1999.

Roberts, Randy *Papa Jack: Jack Johnson and the Era of White Hopes*, Robson Books, 1992.